SALMON
and
SEA TROUT FISHING

SALMON
and
SEA TROUT FISHING

EDITED BY

Alan Wrangles

WITH CONTRIBUTIONS BY
John Chandler, FZS
W G Hartley, BSc, MIBiol, DipRMS, FZS
Conrad Voss Bark

AND ILLUSTRATED BY
Brian Robertshaw

DAVIS-POYNTER
LONDON

First published in 1979 by
Davis-Poynter Limited
20 Garrick Street London WC2E 9BJ

Copyright © 1979 by Davis-Poynter Limited

ISBN 0 7067 0229 8

Photoset by
Bristol Typesetting Co Limited
Barton Manor St Philips Bristol
and printed by
The Stellar Press
Welham Green Hatfield Hertfordshire
Designed by Paul Minns

To Hildegard

Contents

CHAPTER ONE

Review of Present Position of Salmon and Sea Trout Stock

Gilbert Hartley, BSc, MIBiol, DipRMS, FZS

Any consideration of the state of the stock of salmon at the present time has to take account of its previous condition, and the changes in the cultural pressures which affect it. To say that it is rare is not significant if it was never common, and scarcity of numbers does not inevitably presage extinction. By and large, extinction comes to a species from accidental and unpredictable causes. It is true that there seems to be a biological antagonism between the human species and the salmon, but the odds seem to be moving in the direction of favouring the fish in the prospect of ultimate survival.

The salmon appears to suffer more than most regulated species from ignorance, greed and prejudice, which provide the foundation on which the accepted conservation system rocks unsteadily. While it will be agreed without serious dissent that the salmon, along with all other native animals, ought to be safeguarded, this altruism comes a very bad also-ran in the race for drinking water, power, sewage, and commerce. Those responsible for protecting the stocks of migratory fish—which include sea trout, eels and twaite shad as well as salmon—have to walk like Agag to preserve a national asset, the financial significance of which does not compare with the profit to be had by abandoning it.

While it must be accepted that ultimately the position will arise in which our taps continue to run, our cisterns flush and our lights burn, when there is no food and nothing outside the house to draw us forth, this Utopian hell is still a long way off, and can be postponed by considered action. Come it will eventually, if our own species persists; the

effect on all other forms of life is inevitable. To paraphrase
Socrates' argument; 'Would you rather have a salmon than a
bath? Would you rather have a salmon than heating?' The
more pertinent question would be 'Will you pay for your
own amenities?'—and the answer is a crashing 'No!'

The history of salmon conservation in Britain is a very
long one, with a fascinating array of victories and reverses.
Like most long histories, it is encrusted with myths and
nonsense, inspiration and treachery, neglect and downright
persecution. Over the centuries the antagonists have
changed, and ignorant recklessness has given way to system-
atic denial of needs.

The idea of ignorance has been emphasized because
ignorance is at the root of all salmon problems. It might be
thought that a culture which can send trippers to the moon
would have little difficulty in compiling a comprehensive
knowledge of a fish confined to the northern coasts of one
ocean, and of semi-automatic habits at that. The reason for
the difference is financial; space research has gigantic funds
and a correspondingly developed organization, while salmon research ranks as a beggar —and a beggar who ought to
be usefully employed at that—lodging in corners and
passages of institutions mainly engaged in more serious
activities.

From time to time some commercial wound erupts—
salmon are imported from novel sources, disease assumes
plague proportions, new catching practices are introduced
—and administration turns to the fishery scientists for an
immediately operable programme of counter-measures.

The advice given is never based on a scientific appraisal of
the problem, because the essential background of reliable
data is totally lacking, but on the personal judgment based
on long experience of a group of those best fitted to express
an opinion.

A scientific investigation is normally started to provide
data for a future occasion, but scientific investigations on
salmon suffer from the fact that the salmon life-cycle is
about three years at least, whilst the duration of political
interest is not only shorter, but subject to violent changes.
The result inevitably becomes an accumulation of half-

completed research projects, which are absorbed by those involved and incorporated into their fund of experience.

There are no 'experts' in this field, properly speaking, but a number of individuals whose opinions are worth attention, and become less fallible with age, but never infallible.

This method is in sharp contrast to that practised in the case of the Pacific salmon, a fish associated with the Fraser River, the stock of which is fished by the United States and Canada. The operational fishing is under the control of an International Commission which must be one of the most effective in the world. Long collection of accurate data enables trouble to be recognized instantly, and the entire fishing operation can be stopped short within twenty-four hours should there be a discrepancy between the day's catch and its forecast value.

The Pacific scientists have the advantage of working with fish which run as accurately as a railway, but even with this advantage, and without an international complication, the whole fishery could be chaotic and fished to extermination if under the auspices of a number of partially-concerned departments.

The explanation of this admirable state of affairs is that in the great rivers of western Canada and the United States, salmon are big business—very big business indeed—and it is in the common interest that nothing should endanger the breeding stock. An appalling warning was received in 1913, when the major breeding run was eliminated by obstruction due to railway works in the Fraser Gorge, and this has provided as its legacy a most complete and constructive body of ascertained information on the promotion of the fish and their interests.

Even in Britain there is a marked difference between the approach to salmon in Scotland and England. Ignoring angling, which in spite of its prestige value and popular envy has about as much significance to the salmon system as the froth on a glass of beer, salmon fishing in Scotland is big business, operated and controlled by a few large companies with an eye to the future.

In England it is a cottage industry, followed by individuals using traditional or extemporized equipment. The

results show in the annual reports of catches, which have
been mandatory since the original Salmon Commissioners
investigated the decline of salmon stocks over a century ago.
The Scottish figures, which are supplied by the big companies and derived from their trap-nets, provide a reasonably reliable record of the fish caught, though detailed
information is kept in confidence for some years to avoid
commercial rivalry.

The English and Welsh figures, collected from the
individual fishermen and fitted into the contemporary
grouping of areas first by the Fishery Boards, then the River
Boards, then the River Authorities and latterly the Water
Authorities—a succession achieved within thirty years—
represent only such fish as cannot prudently be disclaimed.
An independent fisherman has to make a profit in spite of
the vagaries of weather and rising costs of gear, and he will
not willingly pay more income tax nor encourage the
Authority to increase his licence fee or a fishery owner his
rental. The consequence is that the figures painstakingly
included in the annual reports are of the flimsiest value to
those engaged in protecting the fishery. Over a century they
provide startling evidence of the changes in what is called a
good or bad season, but as a means of following changes
they are at best suspect and at worst misleading.

One reason for this unsatisfactory state of affairs, quite
distinct from numerical inaccuracy, is that the Atlantic
salmon is incomparably more individualistic than the Pacific.
Not only does it enter the rivers in every month of the year,
but the size of the annual runs in any river varies wildly and
with no discoverable sequence. In these circumstances it is
virtually impossible to ascribe any cause to an observed
effect, or to forecast the result of a recorded situation; there
are too many links in the chain.

From spawning to hatching, from hatching to feeding, from
fry to migratory phase are all distinct epochs with distinct demands on the environment, which is the river. This stage of
the life cycle is under possible observation, and vulnerable to
human mismanagement. From the migratory stage in which
the little fish descend to the sea, to the migratory stage in
which they re-enter coastal waters on their way home, they

are out of human control, and until recently had only their natural foes to evade. Nevertheless, these natural foes accounted for some 96 per cent of the fish between their entry into the sea and return to the river. It is generally thought that the bulk of the loss takes place very soon after the smolts enter the sea. Whether or not there is physiological stress after the transition to salt water can be argued to either conclusion, but the fact remains that initially the salmon is small, and thus liable to be eaten by fish which could not tackle it a month later.

At the other end of its voyaging, it sometimes carries parasitic worms in the intermediate phase. These are not finally salmon parasites; they are quiescent until their ultimate host shall eat the salmon. Their presence implies that there is some predator capable of taking twenty-pound fish in the open ocean, and that it is common enough to provide the parasite with a working base for its life pattern.

In the coastal areas and river mouths, the adult fish are attacked by seals, but this is not a ubiquitous hazard. From this stage on to spawning, the human species is the greatest, and virtually the only, enemy, both by direct aggression and by the biologically cynical act of deprivation of the means of living.

The present state of salmon stocks is thus a subject very difficult to pronounce upon, but one which offers plenty of evidence to judge proposed changes in environment. Water flow, pollution, obstruction, exploitation, are recognizable actions under human control; the important point is to keep their effects in balance, and to know how far any pressure can be applied safely.

Salmon in Britain came under pressure in Roman times, when water mills were first erected and obstructions thus introduced. No doubt their use as fish traps followed immediately, but the scale of the obstruction could not have been sufficient to harm the species even without the saving effects of flooding. Medieval agriculture would have had only a slight impact on the salmon rivers, except where flax-retting occurred, and it is likely that the toxic effects of the effluent were even exploited as occasion offered. It is probable that in the centuries preceding the Civil War,

when alterations in agricultural practice were rejected even
when obviously advantageous,the yearly pattern of salmon
behaviour could have furnished an intelligible guide to the
factors operating. At all events, those concerned were in no
doubt as to the evils of obstructions.

The earliest English fishery legislation, incorporated in
Magna Charta in 1215, deals with the erection of illegal weirs
and fish traps in rivers, and ordains their removal. Obviously
the trouble was recurrent, as similar legislation was re-
enacted periodically until 1923, by which time the danger
had undergone a subtle alteration which remained unrecog-
nized.

This insistence on the free passage of salmon upstream
can easily be mistaken for a piece of medieval protective
legislation, but in fact nothing could be further from the
intention. Salmon fishery was a highly-prized right of great
financial value. The fish themselves came from the sea by
Divine direction for the benefit of mankind—or of such men
as were entitled to them—without breeding or growing up.
Those not caught died and drifted ashore after the winter; it
was a one-way pilgrimage.

Although Izaac Walton seems to have subscribed to the
view that smolts were possibly young salmon, and in fact
this must have been recognized, it was not until the
Stormontfield Experiment in the last century that the
matter was proved, and the necessity to protect smolts for
the benefit of the fishery became inescapable. The medieval
legislation was solely to prevent a downstream weir-builder
denying fish to those upstream, with the inevitable consequence of local violence.

At all events, the serious view taken of these weirs and
traps shows that by the Middle Ages human activity was in a
position to damage the salmon stock very severely, if not to
exterminate it. Traps in rivers are dangerous; they can
eliminate the breeding stock completely if used without
discrimination, whereas angling, whether fair or foul, can
only produce detrimental results in the most extraordinary
situations. It is possible that a weir-fisher might restrain his
depredations to comform with his available market, but fish
could be preserved by salting; the physical difficulty of

transport would probably be the limit to fishing, as there was considerable traffic in salted salmon and sea trout between Northumberland and Paris when the railways opened the way.

The development of suitable rivers for milling, which started seriously in the seventeenth century, could have had a catastrophic effect, but this was averted because men could not easily work at night. Rivers such as the Test, Itchen and Avon were carefully divided by weirs to provide milling heads of 5 feet, to run undershot wheels, for much of their length. The work was carried out expertly and on a comprehensive scale, extra channels being excavated and cross-connected so that a river such as the Test at Romsey rarely has less than three channels, each dammed by brick weirs with culverts controlled by sluices.

A salmon can, in good conditions, swim under a sluice when the head is not greater than 2 feet, corresponding to a water velocity of 6 feet per second for a short distance. A mill working at 5 feet head would thus represent an obstruction incapable of passage. Should the mill run down the level of the head pond, passage would be possible, but no miller would leave a sluice open when he was losing head, and his natural instinct would be to leave them shut overnight to ensure maximum power in the morning. This habit was taken care of by the legal provision that hatches must be drawn after working hours and at week-ends to permit fish to pass.

This benevolent intention was maintained in the Salmon and Freshwater Fisheries Act of 1923, where the relevant sections appear in a haze of round-headed arches of rose-coloured brick, with wooden sluices, and much of the wording comes straight out of earlier centuries, to the mystification of modern lawyers.

In fact, by 1923 the impact of weirs and milling had assumed an altogether more dangerous dimension owing to the use of turbines for electrical generation, and this activity was accepted as milling for the purposes of the Act. It was possible therefore to justify the perpetual denial of water to a fish-pass on the grounds that work was continuing day and night through the week, and in one case that the turbine

provided power to blow the organ in the local church on
Sunday as well.

The 1923 Act provided for the construction of an
officially-approved fish-pass in every new weir, and in every
old one rebuilt to more than half its extent, but restricted
this by the warning that no injury must result to the milling
power—a Utopian concept only realized in times of flood.
Relief has come not through the Fisheries legislation but
from commerical pressures; it is cheaper to take mains
electricity than to generate one's own as a rule, and the
charges for the use of river water can be made to bring the
point home.

In Scotland the situation has been somewhat different,
and requires to be considered from another angle. Fish
passage has been a continuing concern of the Scottish
authorities, whose annual reports dealt at length with the
design of salmon passes, when the English ones appeared to
be interested solely in the financial value of fisheries, like a
modern Doomsday Book. The main Scottish obstructions a
century ago were legal, and concerned the rights to the fish
ascending to a newly-opened water. Then followed the
disastrous Grampian Hydro-electric Scheme, which, with
the engineering facilities available after the First World
War, tunnelled through mountains to intercept and divert
rivers for power generation, creating a desert of empty river
beds, with a complete disregard for the environment.

It was the experience of this episode which led to the very
heavy emphasis on fisheries and the integrity of water
bodies, which marked the setting up of the North of
Scotland Hydro-electric Board. Mistakes were made here,
but they were made in good faith, and the lessons learned
were applied as the scheme progressed. Any power dam is
bad, but given proper facilities the fish stock will, in time,
become adapted to the new situation; there is always a fall in
numbers for a period of years, but then they pick up again—
a phenomenon now observable.

The chief danger with fish-passes at power dams is that a
plan has to be produced before the structure is built, and
until this has been done it is impossible to identify the local
factors which make one pass mediocre, and another a

success. Consequently they present an evolutionary series, with the perfect pass always remaining to build in the next dam—if that is built itself.

The traditionally calamitous pressures on salmon stocks —and indeed on all fish—have been overfishing and pollution. In the case of the salmon, with its perennial urge to migrate up-river when at its highest peak of edibility, over-fishing is fatally easy by simple means, and its existence obvious only when it has taken effect. A complete bar to upstream migration will not begin to show for three years, and at the end of five will have virtually extirpated the stock. The salmon, with its biologically suicidal attachment to its native river and its low return proportions, is particularly vulnerable to reduction in numbers, and once a stock has actually vanished its regeneration requires a massive stocking programme, carried through in the face of the non-migratory fish which will have occupied the vacated biological niche of the salmon parr, and of the exploiters who can insist that as the river is no longer frequented by migratory fish, it is legally open to every form of obstruction, pollution, gravel digging, water abstraction or other profit-able vandalism which was barred by the presence of even a token salmon population.

Destructive fishing is associated with obstructions where the run can be trapped—a situation which has passed into history except for a very few historic sites which are operated on a restricted basis, and would at once be made illegal if properly exploited. The occasional salmon trap associated with a weir is sometimes used for collecting fish for hatchery purposes, and the netting of salmon in non-tidal waters is a thing of the past.

Nets operate in estuaries and along the coast, but their effect is variable. In a dry season, with shoals of fish cruising around waiting for a spate, the catch may be heavy; in bad weather the boats will be unable to fish, and the river will be attractive. The effectiveness of the weekly close-time de-pends on the weather pattern, and it is this which leads to much of the bitterness between the anglers and netsmen, the one observing only the times when the weekend is unsuit-able for fish to run, so that the nets have a bonus on

Monday, and the other the occasions when rough weather
all week dies away during the close-time.

Of the two, it is the anglers who have the duty of guarding
the nursery at no little expense for the commercial gain of
the netsmen, who traditionally consider that their efforts
will not affect the future catch. The economic justification
for all salmon conservation is the commercial value of the
catch, which is off-set against the expense of refraining from
raping the river. It is fortunate that it was at the start of the
century that the commercial nets fished the Wye to virtual
extinction; the Fishery Board was able to buy the almost
worthless fishing rights, rehabilitate the river, and then
operate the fishery on a rational basis, as they had accurate
data on the net catches and could adjust the pressure to
avoid over-fishing, while it earned money for improvements.

This is a particularly fine example of the value of obtaining accurate data on catches, without which, conservation
can become an exercise in chasing a will-o'-the-wisp. One
of the most familiar experiences on the official side, is a
deputation from a small salmon river coming to complain
that something must be done to arrest the decline of the
catch. This may have fallen in successive years from 930 to
701, 820, and now 633—the pattern is obvious. The difficulty in pin-pointing the trouble lies in the fact that in the
past century the catch has varied between 2,004 and 89, with
a long-term average of 490.

The relative parts played by netting, dry weather, severe
floods, frosts, poaching, pollution and other unrecorded
pressures are often impossible to reconstruct, and present
pressures, including water abstraction, land drainage, and
road construction, are altering the base-line so that a normal
set of conditions becomes an academic abstraction. We are
now approaching the position in which anxious fishermen
can be told the number of fish which have entered the river
month by month, but why these are caught or refuse to be
caught must remain a problem solely for the anglers.

The newly introduced practice of fishing for salmon on
the high seas has presented a threat no less severe than
mystifying. Salmon in the Baltic form a closed community

which does not stray into the open sea. The fish are all artificially spawned and reared to smolt stage in Sweden, and circulate in a clockwise direction in the Baltic. In this closed area they are fished successively by the inhabitants of the coastal states, mainly as under-yearlings, and the survivors return to the Swedish coast to be caught, or trapped for spawning purposes. The marine fishery is conducted both with nets and floating long lines, and has been peculiar to the Baltic for many years.

The first alarm that salmon would suffer from extra-territorial fishing came when fish began to be exported from Greenland, though these were caught in Greenland territorial waters in a perfectly reasonable way. The odd thing was that although coastal fishing off Greenland was of immemorial standing, there was no previous information about salmon being available there, though it was accepted that the fish returned to Britain from the north-west.

It may be that changing climatic patterns have taken the fish sufficiently close inshore for their presence to be recognized in the region. The coastal fishing was followed by a rapidly increasing drift net fishery on the high seas, which was particularly alarming because reliable information both on the catch and the effect on British catches was lacking.

The fish caught were in their feeding phase, and could be hooked as well as netted, so that a technique could be based on established cod-fishing practice. Tagging experiments proved that British fish went to Greenland, and that fish tagged in Greenland returned to both Britain and Canada. A great deal of research was devoted to distinguishing the eastern and western Atlantic breeds of salmon in the Greenland catch—there are variations in the blood groups between the two sides.

In view of the complete inability of the nations to operate a system to prevent overfishing herring in the North Sea, the prospects for a rational salmon fishery outside territorial limits appeared minimal, but the position was stabilized and a cessation enforced by protective counter-action by the United States. No doubt some high seas fishing still takes place, but its scale is minimal.

The remarkable thing about the episode was that statistics revealed no effect on the British catch which could with certainty be ascribed to the high seas fishing. The 96 per cent of salmon which failed to return to their rivers seem to provide a buffer capable, at least initially, of absorbing the extra depredation.

Salmon have only rarely been caught at sea apart from this sudden fishery. Trawlers on the Dogger Bank occasionally take sea trout, and the odd salmon was caught off Scotland. Presumably the extinct Rhine salmon and the fish from the west Swedish coast followed the Rhine channel, and kept off the shallow western bottom. Any fish from the Thames will be very instructive.

Beyond doubt the most devasting factor in reducing salmon to the status of an endangered species has been pollution. From the inevitable use of brooks to carry away domestic sewage, to the industrial use of rivers to remove waste material, the process went unchecked until the Thames became a foetid sewer in London during the nineteenth century under the load of some tenth of the inhabitants of England. The Tyne, which had been first among English salmon rivers, was closed to migrating fish; the Trent, Ribble, the Taff, and other rivers traversing industrial areas, notably the Silver Clyde, were inhabited only by fish which did not migrate through the estuaries.

There was a bitter war between polluters, who gained financially, and those who had no financial stake, but a sense of outrage at desecration, which was rarely a legal right to relief. Many of the polluters were local authorities, who argued that sewage treatment would increase the rates, and whose representatives on River Authorities fought proposed improvements for this reason.

The Department of Scientific and Industrial Research joined with the Ministry of Agriculture and Fisheries to study the pollution of the River Tees, and superintended the demise of the salmon stock. The salmon became extinct in the Tees, but in dying out it provided information which was instrumental in understanding and counteracting the effects of pollution in the future. By the end of the 1930s, it was technically possible to treat any industrial waste to render it non-toxic, and the variations of oxygenation in water formed a coherent pattern.

Pollution prevention always receives a set-back in war-time, but the recovery from the necessary acquiescence in a fall of standards was aided by the pre-war experience, and also by a softening of the public conscience, so that the map of fishless rivers, which were formerly to be found wide-spread in the land, has shrunk to a small patch in the Potteries, and brooks which once ran with acid are now spawning streams.

The Thames itself is now ripe for the re-introduction of salmon, and the Tyne stock has gradually recovered. Both rivers have changed during the fishless years, however. The Thames has for over a century had no need for fish-passes, and is now sectionally barred by forty-four weirs built without regard for migrants. The Tyne has been used to supply gravel for construction in the North-East, with the result that its bed has been lowered many feet in the lower stretches, and the foundations of bridges stand up like weirs to prevent fish passing except in heavy flood; much of the spawning area has been dredged out.

It is instructive to notice in both cases that the failure of the salmon stock was due not to the impossibility of adult fish entering the polluted river, but to the poisoning of the migrant smolts on their way out. The Tyne estuary is relatively straight and deep, and the inflowing tide runs under the estuarial water, which at one time was devoid of oxygen from some way above Newcastle to well down the tideway. It was possible for adult salmon to come up with the tide, keeping below the polluted water, and finally to surface into the clean river water overlying the polluted layer, and escape upstream. The smolts migrating down-stream, however, had to leave the clean water and were poisoned in the airless tideway unless a severe flood coincided with their migration period.

The Thames estuary is a winding one, with much more complete mixing of the tidal water and river water, so that conditions are more homogeneous. The effect of the ebb and flow is to move the mixed water like a piston up and down stream; the figure of three weeks has been given for

the transfer of an object from Teddington to the open
sea.

As far as traditional pollution is concerned, therefore, the
battle is going in favour of the salmon, though there are
isolated circumstances in which local unemployment makes
it expedient to sanction the release of a toxic effluent into a
river as the price for expanding a factory.

It is the proliferation of new types of pollutant which is
the modern problem. The detergents which have largely
superseded soap initially caused chaos at the treatment
works by clogging filters with foam, and by continuing to
foam at every weir when discharged into a river. Agreement
on the composition of detergents brought this under
control, but surface-active agents of that type commonly
have a devasting effect on microscopic life; as a rule it is not
the oil from a wrecked tanker which damages fish, but the
detergent used to clean up the mess.

The chemical industry which has given us detergents and
selective weed-killers and insecticides—all excellent in their
intent—has provided the problem of casual pollution of
water bodies by chemicals which have been used on land,
and are of no further interest to the user. A famous case of
this was the poisoning of streams in eastern America by the
washings of DDT sprayed by aircraft on forests to control
spruce bud-worm infestation, but this is only a modern
instance of the pre-war fish mortalities caused by toxic road
tars washing off the surface into streams.

The principle is familiar—the scale of toxicity is different.
Whereas thirty years ago toxicities were reckoned in parts
per thousand, effects now involve doses in fractions of one
part per million. The means of chemical analysis have kept
pace with the demand, though naturally enough they are
more costly and demand more expert handling, but as is inevitable in such a progression, the improvement in measurement and statistical analysis of results reveals the deleterious
effects of elements which were always considered as irrelevant, and occur in detectable quantities in productive
waters. Added to this has been the realization that such a
familiar poison as ammonia differs in its toxicity according
to its degree of ionization, and that in common with other

chemicals, its effect may be enhanced or mitigated by the presence of other toxic substances.

In the circumstances, the fish toxicologist is smothered in his own data, and the perfectly reasonable requirement that permissible levels of pollution should be officially prescribed to protect manufacturers tends to become more Utopian annually. However, the self-styled ecologists who protest at every contamination of pure water do not have it all their own way; nothing will live in distilled water, and the fish of the Scottish granite streams and lochans are stunted from their lack of dissolved material, and thus food.

Mortalities of fish may be due to disease as well as pollution. In the past it was notorious that few specimens were as unforthcoming as a dead fish. One obvious reason for this was that fish were not noticed until they floated, by which time examination was unlikely to be instructive except in cases of gross parasitism. The modern commercial interest in game-fish culture in the United States has radically altered the almost medieval techniques used in the past to maintain healthy stocks in hatcheries, and massive experimental programmes to identify the needs of growing fish and the optimal feeding patterns and diets, have played no small part in the development of strains of trout and Pacific salmon which could be called grotesque. The present interest in fish-farming may safely be expected to provide a body of solid knowledge on diseases affecting game fish; on the Continent carp have felt the benefit of the new systen of physiological therapy, and with the ubiquitous nature of the pond-fish industry, this has led to international regulations on the certification of transported fish to prevent the spread of infective pancreatic necrosis, haemorrhagic septicaemia, and a variety of supposedly virus diseases.

The value of such regulations depends on the altruism of the supplier. No conscientious seller of salmon ova could sign a declaration that the eggs come from parents which have never been exposed to contact with the IPN virus, and a certificate that a consignment of freshwater fish are free from whirling disease is no guarantee that this will not appear within two days.

One of the most alarming outbreaks of disease among

salmon was the pre-war epizootic of furunculosis. This occurred in rivers all over Scotland and England, leading to heavy losses, and occasioned the setting-up of a special committee to study it. The reports of the Furunculosis Committee are clear and scrupulous; they identified a causative bacterium, noticed a number of other diseases which had not been recognized, and studied the origins of the outbreaks; arguments were brought forward for and against infection of the salmon at sea. In fact, every outbreak followed re-stocking from an infected hatchery.

On the Continent, the disease is regarded as endemic, and in Britain it seems to have lost its virulence. A reservoir of infection exists among trout, and this is probably beneficent in that it results in immunity being acquired by all susceptible fish.

This acquisition of immunity brings the pathogen into balance with the fish, so that both can live their lives without either exterminating the other. It has recently been argued that the devastating plagues of antiquity have become reduced in this way to the status of childhood ailments in the course of five human generations, while retaining their power to exterminate populations new to them.

At the end of the last century, the Salmon Plague, otherwise called the Black Cap Disease from the characteristic appearance of the head, threatened to exterminate the stock of salmon. It appeared in some rivers, scattered around the country and not necessarily contiguous, and the mortality was alarming. The condition was studied scientifically and associated with the fungus Saprolegnia and a number of bacterial species, typically found also in water. Over the years the plague diminished in virulence, and by 1910 it was unknown. By 1930, at the time of the Furunculosis Committee, it was felt that the earlier investigation had suffered from the poorly-developed contemporary technique and lack of collected data, so that no definite cause could be accepted for the plague, and *Bacillus salmonis pestis* itself came under suspicion as a real organism.

In the 1960s, a new salmon plague was recognized in Ireland, and under the name of *Ulcerative Dermal Necrosis*, spread to the rivers of England and Scotland. In the light of modern techniques, it proved extraordinarily difficult to find a causative organism or virus, and the name referred to the symptoms, commonest of which was ulceration of the head. Reference to the old reports disclosed a remarkable similarity to the Salmon Plague, even to the pattern of distribution, and W. J. M. Menzies, who was the only authority to have seen the earlier outbreak, considered both to be the same. Meanwhile it proved impossible to transmit the condition with certainty in experimental conditions, and there is evidence that fish recover from it now.

We may therefore accept the proposition that salmon will not be exterminated by disease, though they will undoubtedly suffer catastrophically from time to time as immunity is lost or a new pathogen evolves. Fish pathology and physiological studies will nevertheless play a useful part in identifying the conditions which impose a stress on the fish which enables an otherwise neutral organism to acquire a damaging ascendancy—a state of affairs which will become far commoner as intensive salmon culture develops.

The great hazard is concentration, which permits pathogens to be transferred from fish to fish instead of being washed away downstream; the Furunculosis Committee identified as foci of infection, pools below difficult obstructions, where fish were concentrated when conditions were unsuitable for running the fall.

The increasing and immediate peril to salmon in Britain is lack of water. For many years now the demand for domestic and industrial water has resulted in the removal of water from rivers, and a consequent reduction in their natural flow. In earlier periods this abstraction took place in the most destructive manner, with the construction of reservoirs in the headwaters, from which the abstraction was piped away. This not only drowned spawning ground but also deprived the river of all but a niggardly trickle which the undertakers were forced to concede for farming and amenity purposes. On the whole, the salmon is a fish of the larger rivers; the sea trout will run up brooks and even jump into drains, but salmon tend to frequent the larger rivers. Evolutionary experience may have adapted local stocks to

some northern rivers which are either dry or in spate, but
they move when the flow is high, and a river kept artificially
in drought conditions may be expected to lack attraction for
its stock, which will be more vulnerable to local netting
while they await a rise in the river.

In early years, much hope was reposed in artificial spates,
released from reservoirs to lure salmon into rivers—a typical
engineering concept. In fact, the discharge of millions of
gallons of water for short periods does not usually produce
any notable rise in level at the mouth of the river and may
very well repel fish. We may assume that even water released
from the bottom of a storage reservoir will pick up oxygen
as it goes downstream, and be recognizable as water by fish,
but a spate picks up every manner of other soluble material
in its progress. Notoriously one of the commonest fish-
killers is a sudden thunderstorm, bringing into the water
debris with a high oxygen demand which suffocates the fish.
A designed spate will not wash fields off into the river, but
the average salmon runs on a falling flood, when the river has
been cleaned, and the water freed from the grosser contami-
nants. A quick rise and fall is less attractive whether it is
artificial or due to successful land-drainage. It seems that a
certain continuity is required—the fish perhaps waits to
make sure that the condition is serious and not a flash in the
pan.

Modern abstraction practice is improved to the extent
that the water is left in the river until the last moment, and
abstracted at the tidal limit. This ensures among other
things that a sharp watch will be kept on the water quality
throughout the catchment. In the simpler, or first stage of
such an undertaking, abstraction takes water down to an
agreed minimum flow, which is allowed to escape. As a rule
this condition is reached in stages, with a diminishing
abstraction as the flow lessens, and as it rises a limit is set by
the intake pumps so that floods are scarcely affected and fish
are attracted freely. In some cases, abstraction is permitted
to a very low minimal flow, and a fish pass is supplied by
water pumped from the estuary downstream. This arrangement does not seem to be very attractive in practice.

As the demand for water increases, the tidal abstraction is

stabilized by constructing a regulating reservoir at the head of the river. This enables floods to be caught and held, while the abstraction rate is unaffected by low flows, and maintained at its peak by keeping the river flow topped up to the required level to permit this.

Obviously, the result will be an outflow as steadily at the minimum permissible level as can be managed, though storms in the valley will provide flash floods. It must be anticipated that in the end the only water allowed to escape will be that quantity sufficient to keep a fish-pass running during the upper part of the tidal cycle, and that by then sea trout will have practically taken over from salmon, as they will run in low water conditions.

In the meantime, however, salmon can in principle thrive—and with the benefit of intelligent conservation in the river, which means not restricting angling, but minimizing dangerous situations, and in particular ensuring that smolts have a safe journey to sea—can multiply.

The danger is that as the environment becomes more artificial, the risk increases that a minor disaster will unbalance the entire ecological structure. A spawning may fail because a full river at spawning time is followed by low water and frost—no uncommon thing in natural conditions — and the reduced hatch of fry will suffer more from predation than usual.

If during smolt migration there is unusual loss at power stations, or to predators in the estuary, the alarm bells ring loud and clear. The divided return of the Atlantic salmon preserves it from the surging population pattern of its Pacific counterpart, where one brood year in four overwhelms the opposition and produces a large return, while the other three are decimated, but everything depends upon a smolt-run so plentiful that predators are sated.

Where up-river reservoirs exist, it is common for the trout in them to form a virtual barrier to smolt migration; in such conditions the practical course is either to rely on a hatchery below the dam, saving the cost of a fish-pass, or to trap descending smolts upstream of the reservoir and transport them past it. Both expedients present some risk, and the choice depends on the circumstances.

The broad answer to the question of the present state of our salmon population is, therefore, in the standard phrase, 'as well as can be expected'. It seems inevitable that ultimately the salmon will become an artificially maintained creature, existing either as an enclosed source of food or as an inhabitant of a kind of aquatic wild-life sanctuary, but at present its well-being is as secure as that of the human race. Pollution is no longer a crippling hazard, over-fishing seems to be not the danger which it at first appeared and disease is a factor unlikely to exterminate the species before it has reacted to it.

The principal hazard is deprivation of water, and in the modern context of protecting wild life, if the species dies out from this cause it will be because men have decided that it ought not to persist. What is needed for its protection is an accumulation of factual information; at present an enquiry into a water abstraction can be told by engineering experts that the catchment extends to x acres with an annual rainfall of y inches, representing a reliable yield of z million gallons per day. Asked what minimal residual flow will suffice to protect fisheries, the fishery representative can give no such authoritative opinion, and indeed, the greater his experience the less dogmatic he can be, as he can recall exactly opposite results in various cases, arising from conditions not immediately relevant to the present one.

There was a time when the only salmon research possible to a restricted Inspectorate was based on the inexpensive practice of collecting scales and reading them to evaluate population structures, along with a certain amount of migration study. Migration study has now become ruinously expensive, but it is possible to count individual fish passing a suitable point, and to correlate movement with water temperature, river flow, dissolved oxygen, and any other parameter either obviously relevant or found to be so in hindsight. We are beginning to know what we are talking about, and the salmon will be the beneficiary.

A very important advantage here is that regional water authorities exist on a scale sufficient to allow them to include specialists on fisheries, water availability and pollution, so that a close watch can be kept on local situations by people whose duty goes further than immediate expediency. Although cataclysmic changes in the nature of the authorities have been far too many to permit the specialists to discover their natural communities of interest, it may not unreasonably be hoped that the position has now been reached where different departments of a single body can regard each other as co-operators rather than obstructive or hostile rival factions. At one time the only income of some Fishery Boards came from water undertakings extracting excessive water under a penalty clause; the danger now is that a comprehensive authority may tend to simplify its administration by relegating fisheries to the remote end of the pecking order as a frivolity only noticed by reason of its puerile attempts to interfere with the progress of really serious projects of greater financial significance. The last enemy is the administrator!

Mention has been made of sea trout, and it is necessary to point out the distinctive characteristics of this fish, which in many ways resembles a salmon, but shows a number of disconcerting differences. In Scottish law, sea trout are salmon; in English law they are distinct. Scientifically they belong to the single species of trout found in Europe. Ecologically they show a broad pattern of behaviour spanning the clear-cut distinction between the sea-going salmon and the riverine brown trout.

Salmon live for a period of one, two, three, or exceptionally, four years in the river as parr before migrating to the sea in the spring. In England, the bulk go as single or two-year-old fish, at a uniform length of about 6 inches. In Scotland the smolt age is normally two or three years, and the length is commonly less at migration. In either case the smolts rapidly clear the estuary and disappear out to sea, where they stay during their first winter. Some will return in the following summer, as grilse, and others at the second winter, followed by small summer salmon in the second summer, large springers in the third winter, and large summer salmon in the following summer. The pattern is standard, and persists for fish which return after spawning; the initial spring or summer habit is maintained.

Sea trout on the other hand do not migrate as smolts at

their first spring. Some remain in the river for two years after hatching, but most for three. At migration they are usually considerably larger than salmon smolts, often 8 inches long and weighing twice as much. They are thus ecologically more expensive than salmon to rear—they stay longer in the river, and take far more away with them. Conversely they bring less back. Many sea trout smolts return later in the same year and over-winter in fresh water; some of them spawn. A number do not actually go to sea at all in their first post-smolt season, but remain in the estuary. These may go to sea in the following year. Characteristically sea trout return to spawn in the summer group, not remaining up river for many months like spring salmon, and losing condition far less in the process. In the spring, the descending sea trout kelts are often in very good shape; they have mended in the river, feeding like brown trout. Unlike salmon, they are not fixed to their native river; kelts tagged in south Devon have been recaptured in the Tweed as fresh fish, though it must be noted that sea trout will often enter a river and leave it again before spawning in another.

Unlike salmon, they frequently enter rivers and move upstream in drought conditions. They are compulsive jumpers, and cases are recorded where they have been provoked by a dribbling drain to jump from a stream and pack themselves into narrow pipes—possibly acting on an olfactory cue.

The wandering habit of sea trout makes it a waste of time to re-stock with them; if conditions are suitable, they will occur naturally. The Beaulieu river in Hampshire was denuded during the war, but recovered a stock of the characteristically large fish without artificial stocking as soon as water conditions again became favourable. The quality of the gravel used by sea trout for spawning may be characterized as nut-sized, in contrast to the fist-sized stones favoured by spawning salmon. The two species thus occupy different spawning localities, the sea trout normally using side streams and salmon the main river.

Although both appear to take the same food, and the smolts migrate at the same period, the salmon smolt run seems to be more abrupt than that of the sea trout. It is interesting to note that a batch of mixed smolts character-istically tagged and released early in the day will form two separate shoals, remaining in their particular positions, with the salmon further from the bank than the trout, until all move away as dusk falls. There is evidently a subtle difference in their preferences. It is not uncommon to have rivers which carry large sea trout but no salmon—the Sussex rivers are examples. However, it is uncommon to find salmon-only rivers; the legend that the Usk has no sea trout is false. The sea trout appears to be hardier in the river than the salmon in the pre-migration stage, but the converse applies in the sea among the adult fish.

Sea trout which have spawned—and most spawn annually once they have started—usually come to exhibit a some-what coarse appearance which at one time led to their active destruction, as it was hoped that by exterminating these 'bull trout' the salmon and sea trout stocks could be improved. As previously spawned salmon sometimes show a development of black spots, it is possible for professional fishermen of vast experience to be deceived in identification, and it is no uncommon thing for a fish to be an obvious salmon at one end, and as equally obvious sea trout at the other, with the scales showing an ambiguous pattern. This is hardly surprising; in fact the wonder is that any salmonids are pure-bred, as at spawning time the water is a perfect soup of spermatozoa originating not only from the male parent but also from the attendant ripe parr, both salmon and trout, and from other pairs of fish and their attendants upstream.

There does not appear to be any fixed distinction between sea trout and brown trout; normally, brown trout are larger than sea trout parr of equal age. It seems probable that of any trout brood, some will remain as brown trout, and others, less successful in feeding, will drop into the estuary or even adopt a quasi-salmon habit; but this does not explain the definite smolt migration, and it seems certain that fish of like habits breed together and produce young with similar ingrained propensities—even to a common type of build among fish of a particular river, despite the wandering habit. The salmon is a fascinating fish, but the sea trout presents a far wider and more complicated range of problems.

Where both salmon and sea trout occur together, complications arise in designing structures for their common use. The planning of a fish-pass for use both in high flows, by the salmon, and low flows, by the trout, is not usually equally successful for both, and may be virtually impossible if there are constraints on the water available.

Automatic counters present problems, less in the identification of fish of widely differing sizes than in affording equal inducements to pass through. Where the sea trout run large and reach grilse dimensions there is as yet no reliable means of telling the two apart, and it is necessary to know the local pattern of migration and to divide the total by experience.

At present sea trout occur all around Britain. They spawn in the rivers of Sussex, where salmon are absent, possibly exterminated in the past by obstructions, but unlikely to prosper now in such small streams. It seems that the fish enter from the North Sea, at least to some extent; the salmon of the Hampshire rivers are reputed to come up Channel from the west. Off Norfolk, sea trout are netted at sea in the summer, but these breed in the north, many in the River Coquet in Northumberland, which seems largely concerned in the circulation of both salmon and sea trout off the east coast.

The sea trout of the Tweed have long been famous for the complexity of their life cycle; it used to be held that the last group on which a scale-reader could feel confident was these, where true springers occur to complicate the issue even further, but the palm of difficulty really has to be conceded to the fish of the Baltic, where the sea trout can reach 50 lb weight.

With their exploratory habit, sea trout naturally populate any stream to which they can gain access, and even make sporadic attempts to penetrate such unlikely rivers as those of Somerset. When pollution in the Glamorgan rivers was mitigated, it was not long before anglers were catching sea trout, and a run of sea trout is the usual signal that a river hitherto closed to salmon is again ready for their occupation. In this connection it is surprising that Teddington weir pool is not full of jumping fish already.

Sea trout enter the estuaries of the rivers flowing into the Wash, though sluices prevent a real penetration. The Humber rivers still suffer from a pollution block, and the Tees also, but the other Yorkshire rivers carry sea trout, which are fished by coastal nets in summer.

In Scotland, where no distinction exists in law, sea trout are ubiquitous, and often large; fish of 15 lb are known. Unlike the salmon, which seems to go far off shore unless returning as a grilse, sea trout seem to remain close to the coast; indeed, when netting them it is necessary to avoid leaving a gap between the net and the rocks, as they move in the seaweed—a habit which may explain their tendency to lose identifying tags, and the frequency with which isolated tags prove to be those of sea trout. With this coastal habit, they may well prove to be relatively immune from over-fishing on the high seas.

While there is no occasion for immediate panic about the future of British stocks of salmon and sea trout, it would be the height of irresponsibility to yield up any defensible ground or to fail to push every advantage to its reasonable limit. The qualifications to the conditions are deliberately chosen, as a minority interest—such as salmon conservation —is damaged by attempts to over-call its hand, and loses public sympathy later, in meritorious cases.

We are all aware by now that the preliminary phase of any philistine activity is the crafty manipulation of public opinion to ensure that the expected opposition is made to appear fatuously unreasonable, and it is only after this that the prospective despoiler emerges into public view, as the guardian of amenities for all the people, not just a selfish clique. It is accepted that life must go on, but it should do so as agreeably as possible. Electricity can be generated anywhere, but salmon only in very restricted localities.

CHAPTER TWO

About Salmon and Sea Trout

John Chandler, BSc, FZS, MIBiol, MIWPC

What is a Sea Trout?
Modern science has its roots in the philosophical revolution
of the late seventeenth century, when men first began to
catalogue and question their natural surroundings, rather
than accepting them as the background to everyday life. At
first the process was descriptive, being only an extension of
the ideas which had been propounded by the Ancient
Greeks, but naturalists quickly realized that the many
varieties of plants and animals could be grouped, according
to their similarities, in a logical scheme of classification.

Many rival schemes were proposed, but it was the
binominal system published by Linnaeus in 1758 in the
tenth edition of his *Systema Naturae* which has formed the
basis of zoological taxonomy to this day. The binominal
system uses two names to describe each species: the first is
the name of the genus, or group, to which the species
belongs, and always has a capital initial; the second identifies
the species within the genus, and is never written with a
capital letter. Like Christian names, specific names may
be shared by several species, but the generic and specific
name together are unique, distinguishing an animal or plant
species from all others. Linnaeus's scheme of classification
was artificial in that it grouped together families of animals
which are now known to be unrelated, but had the advantage of enabling animals to be catalogued in a practical way.

Linnaeus recognized three species of trout in Europe, all
within the genus Salmo, which also included the salmon.
These were *Salmo trutta*, the river trout; *Salmo fario*, the
brook trout and *Salmo eriox*, the sea trout. Controversy has
raged over these divisions ever since.

On the one hand, it has been proposed that many more species can be recognized in nature (in 1866 Gunther was able to distinguish ten separate species of trout from Britian

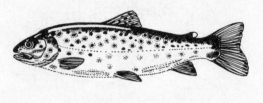

Brown Trout

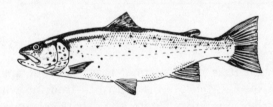

Sea Trout

alone) on the other, it has been suggested that all the European forms of *Salmo trutta* are variations within a single species whose size, form and colouration depend largely on the environment, since all can be made to interbreed to give fertile offspring similar to the parent stock of brown trout.

Sea trout are found in European rivers draining to cold seas between northern Norway and Portugal, but are absent from the Mediterranean and Caspian basins, even though brown trout occur in rivers as far east as the Oxus in northern Afghanistan. Brown trout cannot survive water temperatures in excess of 27°C and do not grow successfully in water warmer than 20°C, so it is probably the presence of high summer temperatures in coastal waters which has prevented migratory trout from developing in the eastern part of the range of the species.

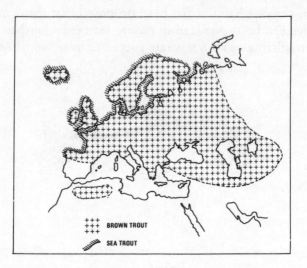

Distribution of Brown Trout and Sea Trout

Although it is now accepted that sea trout are not a separate species, but are distinguished from brown trout only by their migratory habits, the debate continues as to whether they 'breed true' or whether the urge to migrate might be felt equally strongly by any young brown trout, regardless of its parentage. If sea trout are normally the offspring of migratory adults it could be that, as a strain, they are following an evolutionary line distinct from that taken by their sedentary cousins, and could eventually become a distinct and separate species. If this is not the case, then what is it that determines whether a young trout will stay contentedly in its river or brave the hazards of the wider world?

In 1865 a consignment of 103,000 salmon eggs and 15,000 trout eggs was sent to Tasmania packed in ice. Nearly half survived the journey, and some 500 trout fry were reared successfully. From 1868 onwards, the Plenty River into which these fish had been released was established as a natural breeding ground for brown trout in the Southern Hemisphere. Eggs were transferred to New Zealand, and it is significant that as a result the Waiau River in South Island developed a run of sea trout, even though the original eggs sent to Tasmania from Britain had come from non-migratory parent fish. It seems that the urge to migrate is inherent in brown trout, but is triggered by environmental factors.

As long ago as 1910, Dahl found that adult sea trout returning to Norwegian rivers included more female than male fish, even though the sex ratio amongst fingerlings in the river was 1:1, he also noted that the resident population of older brown trout had a preponderance of males, and concluded that young female sea trout migrated out to sea at an earlier age than the males. Similar results were obtained by Alm, working on a Swedish river, and by Piggins in Ireland. It was suggested that the bias in favour of female fish in the adult sea trout run was due to the males being less hardy during their life at sea, but no evidence was available to explain why this might be the case. Workers on the Tyne, Tees, Dovey and Tweed have now found that the imbalance in the sex ratio of returning adult sea trout is also found amongst the smolts migrating out to sea. If more female fish go to sea in the first place it is not surprising that more females return as adults, and no theory of differential mortality is needed to explain the facts.

Recent work in Welsh rivers and on the Tweed in Scotland has shown that the excess male 'sea trout' left in the river after the run of predominantly female smolts, become sexually mature without having to go to sea and are indistinguishable from non-migratory male 'brown trout'. Similar differences have been reported in the sex ratios of the resident and migratory components of other species of salmonids.

In Nova Scotia, 72 per cent of the smolts of migratory brook char (*Salvelinus fontinalis*) were female and 28 per cent male. Those which remained in the river were 29 per cent female and 71 per cent male. Investigation into the char of Kamchatka (*Salmo malma*), kunzha trout in the Black Sea and sockeye salmon in British Columbia have resulted in similar findings, leading to the suggestion that the resident population was the progeny of migratory parents, but that female smolts had a greater urge to migrate than the males. Reviewing this evidence in the light of his work on the River

Tweed, Campbell suggests that the brown trout which
move out of the main river into the tributaries to spawn are
the progeny of migratory parents, and that the sea trout and
brown trout of the River Tweed must be regarded as
members of a single coherent population of fish. It now
seems certain that there is no such thing as a sea trout in
biological terms, there are only sea trout rivers. The factors
which determine if trout will migrate or not remain
unresolved.

What is a salmon?
In contrast to the brown trout, which is a very variable
species, the Atlantic salmon is uniform in shape and colour
over its whole range. In the absence of pollution, *Salmo
salar* is found in cold rivers on both sides of the Atlantic
from latitude 40°N to the limit of coasts affected by winter
pack ice. In European waters its distribution is similar to
that of the sea trout, and it is not found in the Mediterranean
basin. Salmon prefer large rivers which remain cool in
summer, but are also found in smaller rivers such as the
Hampshire Test and Dorset Frome where the summer flow
and temperature are maintained by a high proportion of
water from chalk springs. Smaller rivers with higher summer
temperatures, such as those on the south and east coasts of

Salmon—male and female

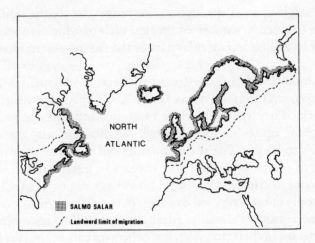

Distribution of Atlantic Salmon

England, are not attractive to salmon, but may support runs of sea trout if their upper reaches are suitable for trout parr.

The existence of the Artic ice cap has prevented the spread of *Salmo salar* into the Pacific Ocean, where its place is taken by fish of the genus *Onchorhynchus*, which is closely related to *Salmo*. In contrast to the Atlantic salmon, which

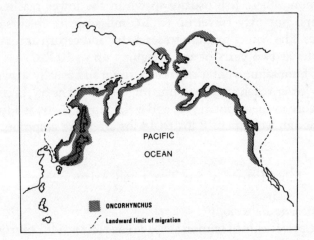

Distribution of Pacific Salmon

is a single species throughout its range, the Pacific salmon have evolved a number of species, each of which is specialized to exploit a particular part of the environment open to it.

Chinook salmon are found in large rivers such as the Yukon, and may travel as far as 2,000 miles upstream to spawn. They enter the river in spring and early summer, weighing up to 108 lbs, although weights generally average 10 lbs to 50 lbs. The young migrate out to sea in their first year of life or after one or two years in freshwater.

Sockeye salmon are also found in large river systems, but will only enter rivers fed by lakes, passing through to spawn in the tributary streams. After hatching, some fry migrate out to sea in their first year, but others mature in the lake for one, two or three years before leaving for the sea. Returning adult fish weigh 5 to 7 lbs, with occasional fish up to 15 lbs.

Coho salmon penetrate into the upper tributaries of large rivers, but may spawn in smaller rivers in the lower reaches just beyond the head of the tide. Most young fish leave freshwater at one year old, but a few stay one or two years longer before migrating out to sea. Mature fish weigh 6 lbs to 12 lbs, but fish in excess of 25 lbs have been recorded.

The mature males of pink salmon develop a large bump on their backs, giving them their alternative name of humpback salmon. These fish usually spawn in the lower reaches of rivers, but may travel up to 200 miles upstream in some cases. The young migrate to sea as fry and return as mature adults at two years of age, weighing up to 10 lbs.

Chum salmon enter rivers in autumn and usually spawn in the lower reaches. The young migrate to sea as fry, become mature in their fourth year and weigh up to 30 lbs as adults, although weights of 8 lbs to 18 lbs are more common.

Life History of Sea Trout and Atlantic Salmon

Spawning Behaviour
The private life of salmon at spawning time was for centuries the stuff of anglers' tales, shrouded in mystery and imagination, but the true facts were revealed by Dr J. W. Jones

following a remarkable series of experiments in the late 1940s. An observation tank with plate glass windows in its walls was built below water level in the bank of the River Alwen, a tributary of the Welsh Dee, allowing observers on the dry side of the windows to watch the behaviour of salmon in the tank, which was fed with river water controlled by sluices at either end. The floor of the tank was filled with about a foot of gravel from a known spawning ground on the river, and water was allowed to flow through for several weeks before ripe male and female salmon were put in at the beginning of the spawning season. Dr Jones found that salmon refused to spawn when the water velocity was reduced to two or three inches per second, but at six times this flow rate they would spawn successfully in only six or seven inches of water. Male and female fish spent a considerable time resting in the pools at either end of the tank, but from time to time a dominant male would nudge a female or bully other males. When ready to spawn, the females were seen to wander over the spawning bed, and then to start cutting a redd in the gravel, accompanied by the dominant male, who would lie quivering beside her. By photographing the process on slow-motion film, it was possible to see that the female cuts the redd by hydraulic pressure, lying on her side facing upstream and flapping her tail vigorously. This results in strong local water currents which lift the gravel and silt beneath her tail, allowing the river flow to displace it downstream. In vigorous cutting movements the body of the fish was seen to be bent into an inverted U, but the fish was prevented from moving forward

Salmon cutting a redd

by the erection of the pectoral, pelvic and dorsal fins, which maintained a grip on the water.

In the early stages of courtship a female salmon would make feeble cutting movements at random over the spawning bed, but having chosen a site for the redd, would direct her activity to a restricted area until a trench had been excavated six inches or more below the bed of the stream. At this stage the male was in attendance, and between bouts of cutting activity the female 'felt' the progress of her digging by trailing her pelvic and anal fins over the bottom of the hole.

Once the trench had been cut, the female salmon was seen to lower herself slowly into the deepest part, with her anal fin erect, and to manoeuvre until her vent lay between two of the larger stones at the bottom. She would then press her body into the hole, raising her head away from the stream bed in a 'crouching'posture, open her mouth and then lay a quantity of eggs. The 'crouch' was seen to act as a signal to the male, who showed signs of excitement and drew closer, until he lay alongside the female. Then, with fins erect, mouth open and opercula expanded he would shed milt over the eggs at the moment they were laid.

Immediately after orgasm, the female salmon was seen to swim a short destance upstream and to start cutting a new spawning bed, displacing stones and gravel to cover the eggs which had just been laid. Not all the eggs were laid in the first bed, and the new trench would frequently become the next spawning bed. 12 lb salmon were seen to dig a succession of up to eight spawning beds a foot or more deep before laying all their eggs.

Female salmon evict intruding females from their chosen spawning area by a ritualized threat display, similarly, dominant male salmon chase other adult males away from the female during redd cutting activity. It appears to be cutting activity which attracts a sexually ripe dominant male salmon to a ripe female, and the quivering of the male which spurs the female on to complete her redd. If the male is removed before the eggs are laid the female will not proceed further. It was found that light intensity was of little importance to spawning salmon. They continued their activities in turbid water and through the hours of darkness, and were not put off by the use of floodlights. Salmon were observed spawing only when the water temperature was between 2°C and 6°C, although spawning activity had been observed in the river up to 10°C. Below 1°C females cut spawning beds only half-heartedly and did not lay any eggs.

The gravel used in these experiments varied between a quarter of an inch and seven inches in diameter and was laid at random on the river bed. Such a mixture has a large percentage of voids through which water can flow, and it was thought that female fish select suitable gravel by detecting the surface texture before cutting began. Spawning behaviour was never observed on the concrete floor of a holding box.

In over ninety spawnings observed in the tank, there was only one occasion when the eggs were washed out by the current, and it was later found that they were laid by a sick fish. The success of fertilization of eggs in the wild was found to be very high, averaging 98.5 per cent in the redds examined. The heavy mortalities suffered by salmon come at a later stage in the life history.

It has long been known that male salmon parr in freshwater may become sexually mature before migrating out to sea, and hatchery experiments have shown that they can be used to fertilize eggs artificially. One of the questions Dr Jones was able to answer using his observation tank, was whether sexually mature male salmon parr are able to fertilize salmon eggs in nature.

Early in the series of experiments with adult fish it had been seen that male parr were very interested in the activities of female salmon cutting spawning beds. They were not tolerated if seen by either of the adult fish, and would be chased away with aggressive behaviour. Their favourite position was seen to be below the female at the bottom of the spawning bed, out of sight of the adults. In the absence of an adult male it was found that female salmon would not spawn with mature male parr, but by substituting sterilized adult males for the original fish, Dr Jones found that spawning activity continued and fertile eggs were produced when the only milt available had been provided by the parr.

At first sight, the evolution of this behaviour appears to be wasteful of the salmon's resources. Why should parr expend energy producing milt when adult males are perfectly capable of fertilizing the eggs? Dr Jones suggests that this must be a form of insurance for the species, with the outside possibility that it may be the first stage in the evolution of salmon which spend their whole lives in fresh water.

Laboratory investigations, using smaller scale tanks, have shown that brown trout, and by inference, sea trout, have very similar spawning behaviour to that of salmon. It is the female who chooses the spawning bed and excavates the nest and the male trout exhibit the same quivering behaviour as the salmon. A 12-inch female trout will take up to an hour and a half to cut a nest ten or twelve inches long and three inches deep, moving upstream to excavate more gravel after spawning in the same way as has been described for salmon.

The sites chosen by salmon and sea trout for their spawning beds invariably consist of mixed gravel, situated in those parts of the stream where there is a flow of water through the stones. This is important for the survival of the eggs, as the flow of water continuously replenishes the oxygen they consume, and also keeps them free from silt. In static water the dissolved oxygen would be used by bacteria feeding on organic matter in the water and the eggs would suffocate. Salmon favour coarser gravel than do trout, but in other respects their redds are similar.

Redds are clearly recognizable in the weeks following the spawning season. By disturbing the stream bed, the adult fish expose gravel which was previously buried and has no coating of diatoms and algae, so that the redd usually appears as a lighter patch against the darker background of the stream bed until it, too, is colonized by microscopic plants. Redd counts are valuable in fishery management, allowing an estimate to be made of the size of the spawning stock of adult fish, but must be made regularly throughout the spawning season so that multiple redds on the same spawning ground can be recognized.

Development of the Embryo
As would be expected from closely related species, the early

lives of salmon and sea trout are very similar, although there are differences of detail concerning optimum water temperature and hatching times. The first hundred days or so of the life of a salmon are spent within the protection of the egg shell, buried deep in the gravel of the stream bed. Newly laid salmon eggs are flabby, and at one point on the surface there is a small pore at the bottom of a conical pit, the micropyle, through which the sperm enters to fertilize the egg. At this stage the eggs rapidly absorb water through the outer porous shell, making them slightly adhesive to the touch. Once this process is complete, the eggshell is tightly stretched by the turgor pressure of its contents giving the egg a spherical shape about a quarter of an inch in diameter, and flattening the micropyle funnel against the inside of the shell so that fertilization after this time is impossible. Eggs are fertilized while being shed into the nest by the female fish. The milt which is shed simultaneously by the male contains very many more sperm than the number needed to fertilize the eggs. Each sperm consists of a 'head' of genetic material and 'tail' which it lashes strongly enabling it to swim towards the egg, to which it is probably attracted by chemical stimuli. The sperm is very much smaller than the egg, but only one is needed to ensure fertilization, and only one may enter via the micropyle.

After entry, it sheds its tail and its nucleus fuses with that

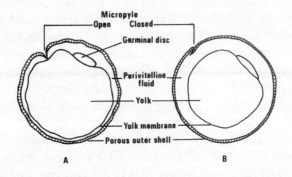

Egg structure of trout or salmon. A. pre-germination and B. post-germination.

of the egg. Since egg and sperm each contain only half as many chromosomes as those in the cell nuclei of the parent fish, after nuclear fusion the fertilized egg contains a full complement of genetic material, half from each parent. Salmon and trout sperm can only survive for about one minute in fresh water, so fertilization must be almost instantaneous as the eggs are laid in the gravel.

Within the porous shell, the egg is almost completely filled by the yolk, which is contained in a thin membrane and separated from the shell by a layer of fluid. The yolk itself is a viscous yellow fluid containing a number of oil drops which congregate in the upper half, under the embryo which is developing on the top surface of the yolk. Because of the fluid layer separating the eggshell and its contents, the whole yolk mass is able to rotate freely so that the embryo is always found at the top of the egg, no matter which way up it falls in the nest.

Because the inside of the egg is isolated from the environment, the embro can only grow by using the food stored within the egg. In effect, the yolk is a survival pack provided by the hen fish to keep her offspring going until they can fend for themselves. Although isolated from the surrounding water, salmon and trout eggs are very sensitive to mechanical shock until they reach quite a late stage of development. Within its membrane, the yolk contains a large quantity of protein which can be kept in solution only in the presence of mineral salts. If the delicate yolk membrane is damaged the salts leak away through the porous egg shell, the protein coagulates into a solid white mass and with its salt balance upset, the embryo dies. As the embryo develops, the yolk membrane is strengthened by the growth of a thicker wall of cells, and by the time the young fish has developed eyes, which can be seen through the shell, the yolk membrane is strong enough to withstand mild mechanical shocks.

Trout eggs hatch successfully at water temperature of between 5°C and 13°C, but outside these limits the mortality rate increases markedly. Salmon can withstand slightly lower temperatures than trout, but for both species the time taken for eggs to hatch decreases with rising temperature, and the optimum range for survival is 8°C to 10°C.

Temperature °C	Days to hatch	
	Salmon	Sea Trout
2	115	148
6	95	77
7	90	68
10	75	41

Time for Eggs to Hatch

As the embryo grows within the egg it can be seen as a light-coloured crescent of tissue overlying the yolk. About two-thirds of the way through the incubation period the

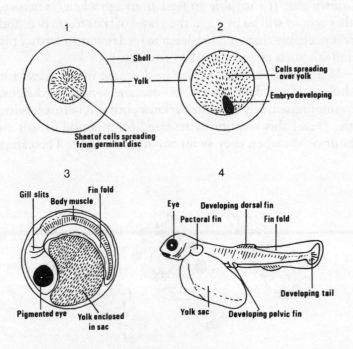

Stages of development of the trout or salmon egg

eyes can be seen as black spots through the eggshell and just before hatching, the alevin, as the embryo is now known, secretes an enzyme which dissolves the inner layer of the shell wall. By wriggling vigorously the alevin ruptures the shell and breaks free into the outside world, where it lies quietly in the darkness between the grains of gravel.

Development after Hatching

Not all the yolk is used by the embryo whilst still within the egg shell. That which remains at the time of hatching is carried by the alevin in the strengthened yolk sac attached to its underside, and is the sole source of nourishment for the developing fish for three or four weeks. As the alevin becomes increasingly more fish-like, the yolk is absorbed until the stage is reached when it is all used up, and the young salmon or trout is known as fry.

Once they have exhausted their yolk reserves, young fry must either feed or perish. From hatchery experience it is known that fry are able to feed at an age when, in nature, they would still be living in the gravel of the stream bed, and it is probable that wild fish learn to feed first on microscopic animals such as protozoa and rotifers.

When first hatched, alevins lie dormant in the gravel for three or four days, then they become sensitive to light, swimming actively towards darkness, but just before leaving the gravel this reaction is reversed for a period of half an hour or so, when they swim towards the light. Thereafter

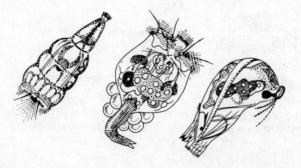

Rotifers

Protozoa

light ceases to be the dominant factor in their orientation, and young fry are most influenced by the direction of water currents, although they will dart into the gravel if disturbed.

On leaving the gravel, trout fry rapidly disperse and choose individual territories which they defend against other fry. The largest, and those which hatch first, have a head start in the struggle for existence which will continue throughout their lives. Weaker fry are not able to hold the best territories and as a result may grow more slowly or be more exposed to predators than their successful brethren. The lessons of life in the wild are hard and are learned at an early age. In contrast to the behaviour of trout, salmon fry tend to stay together in a shoal just above the stream bed and do not take up individual territories.

Newly-hatched alevins are naked and colourless, but as they grow larger they develop pigment cells in the skin, and shortly after losing their yolk sacs, at a length of about an inch, scales begin to appear along the lateral line on each side of the body. Scales first show as minute outgrowths of the skin which eventually grow to form a layer of overlapping bony plates, each encased in a pocket of skin, which cover the body of the fish like slates on a roof. As this happens, the pigment spots and dark vertical 'parr marks' on the sides of the body become more apparent. Like so many terms which have evolved over the centuries from the vocabulary of angling, the definition of what constitutes a parr is open to argument. In general terms, it is a young salmon or sea trout which has not yet changed its coat in response to the call of the sea, and is no longer a fry, but the precise change from fry to parr is difficult to define. Certainly, the fish are still fry until they have all their scales, but that is as far as it is safe to go.

Salmon and trout parr are similar and often confused, but

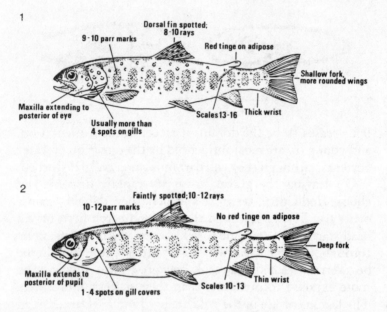

Parr. 1 Trout. 2 Salmon.

can be distinguished if compared carefully. Like twins, it is often easier to identify them when they are side by side than it is if they are seen apart. In trout, the upper jaw bone extends backwards level with the posterior edge of the eye, whilst in salmon it is relatively shorter, reaching only to the back of the pupil. The adipose fin between the dorsal fin and the tail has a red or orange tinge which is lacking in salmon, and the tail, which has rounded wings and is shallowly forked, has a thick wrist where it joins the body. (In adult fish, if you can pick up a sea-trout by the tail, it is a salmon!)

The salmon parr has a tail which is more deeply forked, with pointed wings and a narrow wrist. There are usually ten to twelve parr marks in contrast with trout, which have nine or ten, and salmon parr have fewer than four spots on the gill cover whilst trout have four or more. Although many of these diagnostic features overlap, it is usually possible to use several of them to distinguish between salmon and sea trout parr, but it has recently been discovered that the two species do hybridize to a small extent in the wild, and the fish which fits neither description, or both, may be a cross.

It is interesting to note that for many years salmon parr were thought to be a distinct species of fish known as *Salmo salmulus*, and it was only when they were reared artificially by Shaw in 1840, who was the first man to strip salmon and hatch their eggs, that they were recognized as the young of the Atlantic salmon.

Artificial Rearing of Salmon and Sea Trout

The mortalities suffered by salmon and sea trout over the period of a generation are enormous, and the chances of any one fish surviving to become a parent in its turn are correspondingly small. In a stable population, the number of spawning adults will be the same from year to year, and if each pair spawns only once, only two of their offspring need to survive to maturity to maintain the balance. If more than two survive there will be an increase in the adult population, if fewer than two, the population will decline and may collapse completely.

The number of eggs laid by a female salmon is variable but is related to the logarithm of the fish's length and to its weight. Estimates vary between 400 and 900 eggs per pound of body weight, but the accepted average is of the order of 650 to 700, so a 20 lb hen salmon could be expected to lay a maximum of 14,000 eggs. If only the hen and her mate are to be replaced in the population by their offspring then 13,998 will fail to reach maturity. It was these high losses in the wild which first attracted fishery managers to the idea of rearing salmon and trout artificially, using protected hatcheries to increase the population of adult fish, so that a larger crop could be taken without jeopardizing the survival of the species as a whole.

For this policy to be successful it must be possible for hatcheries to rear more fish of a given age than would have been produced naturally in the wild. The time spent in the hatchery must cover the period of maximum risk in the wild mortality after release should be low, and the size of the adult population in the wild should not be limited by the food supply. In the case of migratory fish, adults should return to the fishery in which their parents were caught, or hatcheries should be established throughout the range of the species so that all who benefit from increased yields also contribute towards the cost of stocking.

In the case of enclosed fisheries, such as those for brown trout in rivers, or the extreme example of put-and-take rainbow trout fisheries in reservoirs, most of these conditions are met, but the position with regard to salmon and sea trout is less clear cut. In particular, mortality in the sea is thought to be high, and in the case of sea trout there is doubt whether the adult fish return to their parental stream. Neverthless, in the wild, only 3 per cent of salmon are likely to survive their first year of life, making hatcheries a viable proposition in those cases where an immediate return on the investment is not required, or where the hatchery operators control all the fisheries in a catchment. A recent commercial development has been the farming of Atlantic salmon in cages in the sea, so that they can now be produced for the market having spent their whole lives in captivity.

Whereas the rainbow-trout breeder can select his broodstock and fatten them up for the spawning season to come, the manager of a hatchery producing salmon or sea trout is dependant on nature for the parent fish he requires and he has no control over their condition or availability.

Adult fish are usually taken from the river as near as possible to the spawning season. This is done because it is difficult to keep them in captivity for any length of time without the risk of outbreaks of disease, which may severely reduce the numbers held. There is little point in nurturing eggs and young fish at the cost of killing off the parents of very many more which might have survived in the wild. Adult fish may be trapped in fixed structures built in the river where a strong flow of water attracts them in their journey upstream.

The mouth of the trap consists of rows of vertical bars, or nets supported on frames, running diagonally across the current in the shape of a V, with the apex pointing upstream. The two arms of the V do not meet, but have a gap between them just large enough to allow a fish to pass into the body of the trap, where its progress upstream is prevented by a cage of bars, withies or netting.

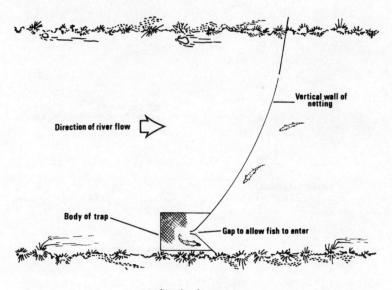

Direction of river flow

Vertical wall of netting

Body of trap

Gap to allow fish to enter

A fixed salmon trap

A more common method of catching parent fish is by the use of seine nets in estuaries or in pools at the head of the tide. The net may be over one hundred yards long and must be deep enough to stretch from the surface to the bottom of the pool when being dragged through the water. It must also have a mesh fine enough not to entangle and damage the catch. One end is made fast to the shore, whilst the body of the net is laid in a half circle from a boat rowed round the area to be netted. When the net is set, both ends are drawn in towards the shore making the circle of netting progressively smaller, and eventually trapping fish in an area small enough for them to be removed by hand.

A third method of catching adult fish is the use of electric fishing machines. These are effective only in fresh water, as the high conductivity of brackish or salt water dissipates electrical energy so fast that a workable generator for use in these conditions would be unmanageably large. The method works by creating electric fields in the water which directly stimulate the fish's nerves and muscles, and this system is most effective with large fish. Control circuits can be designed to attract and immobilize fish, or to stun them at a

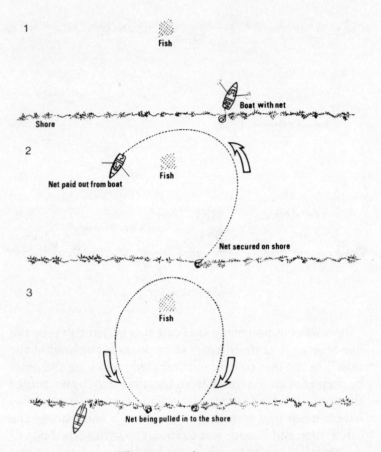

1

Fish

Boat with net

Shore

2

Net paid out from boat   Fish

Net secured on shore

3

Fish

Net being pulled in to the shore

Three stages of seine netting

distance of several yards, but power outputs of the order of
two kilowatts are usually required, so the method is poten-
tially dangerous if used by untrained operators. Because of
its effectiveness as a poaching tool, the use of electric fishing
machines in England and Wales is controlled by the water
authorities.

Holding facilities for adult salmon and sea trout need to
be sufficiently large to prevent overcrowding, with a strong
flow of fresh water to maintain the health of the fish, but the
design must be such be such that fish can be easily removed
without damage for inspection as the spawning season

approaches. Pre-spawning salmon and sea trout are in a state of physiological stress, which is not helped when they are confined. Under these conditions outbreaks of fungal skin disease may occur if fish are not treated from time to time with a preventative fungicide such as Malachite green.

Fish are recognized as ripe when light pressure on the abdomen causes milt or eggs to be shed freely from the vent. Great care should be taken when handling ripe fish as they are very easily damaged. In particular, female fish should never be held downwards by the tail, as the weight of eggs is so great that this may cause the ovary to rupture prematurely, releasing eggs into the forward part of the body cavity before they are ready to be shed.

Ripe hen fish are stripped by holding them with the head sloping upwards, and the vent over a suitable bowl or bucket. To expel the eggs, the abdomen is gently squeezed,

Stripping

starting nearest the vent, using a short stroking movement running in the direction from head to tail. It is important that stripping should not be forced, too much pressure may rupture the ovaries, which leads to a lower survival rate of the eggs in the hatchery. It is the eggs nearst to the vent which ripen first, and it may be necessary to strip a hen fish on a number of occasions, a few days apart, if all her eggs are to be obtained in peak condition.

Struggling with a large female salmon whilst trying to strip her eggs gently into a bowl can be more than one or even two men can cope with. Fish can be pacified if their heads are covered with a wet dark cloth, or they can be strapped to a board with broad strips of canvas. This makes the job simpler and less stressful for both the staff and the prospective parent.

Some hatcheries recommend the use of anaesthetics. Fish are placed in water containing a suitable concentration of the appropriate drug, which is absorbed via the gills. Within a few minutes breathing movements cease and the fish turn over onto their backs. At this stage they are stripped of eggs or milt before being returned to fresh water to recover. Although the use of anaesthetics minimizes the risk of mechanical damage caused by the fish struggling, the drug is a hazard to the adult fish, and there is always the danger that anaesthetic will drip from the fish into the bowl containing the eggs. If this happens, it could interfere with the process of fertilization, rendering the whole batch useless. If anaesthetics are used, great care must be taken to rinse the fish with clean water and to dry them with a towel before they are stripped.

Salmon sperm are rapidly inactivated by fresh water, which also causes newly-shed eggs to swell, rendering them incapable of fertilization. For these reasons, eggs are best stripped into a *dry* bowl and fertilized with milt stripped directly from a cock fish. Water should not be added until the eggs and milt have been gently mixed by stirring with a feather. Then they should be rinsed to remove excess milt, and placed in clean fresh water to 'harden off' whilst they absorb water. If great care is taken to exclude all water when adult fish are stripped, it is possible to transport both eggs and milt in chilled, sealed plastic bags from which the air has been expelled, and delay fertilization for up to 24 hours, enabling offspring to be reared from parent fish which it would have been impossible to bring together.

The sensitivity of salmonid eggs to mechanical shock is at a minimum for a period of about 48 hours after fertilization, allowing them to be handled and transported at this time. It is convenient to count eggs before laying them down in incubators by comparing their volume with that of a known number, and it is possible to estimate the success of fertilization of day-old eggs by immersing a sample in 10 per cent acetic acid. Infertile eggs remain clear whereas the embryos in fertile eggs turn white. This treatment obviously kills the eggs tested and cannot be used on the whole egg harvest, but information on the success of fertilization enables the hatchery manager to assess losses from other causes during incubation.

In traditional hatcheries, fertilized eggs are incubated in shallow baskets supported in troughs in a flow of clean water. Many materials have been tried for the construction of the baskets. Early workers used fine mesh netting supported on wooden frames, a technique which has been updated to meet modern requirements by the use of nylon and other synthetic net materials. At one time, baskets were made with bottoms consisting of a horizontal layer of loosely spaced glass rods, or the baskets themselves were dispensed with, and glass rods were laid across the hatching troughs in a layer below water level, so that developing eggs were supported and newly hatched alevins wriggled through the spaces into the water below.

These methods fell out of favour as the cost of replacing glass rods rose, and better synthetic materials were developed. Perforated zinc and galvanized wire mesh have been used for hatchery baskets, but these materials introduce the possibility of zinc poisoning causing egg mortalities in acid waters, which dissolve the metal, although they are acceptable in waters with a pH greater than seven. Today, the material used most often for hatchery baskets is expanded aluminium alloy, either anodized or nylon-coated to prevent corrosion in alkaline water. This material has elongated slots which allows alevins to drop through easily. It is cheap and easy to fabricate.

Eggs are laid down in the baskets, one or two layers deep, allowing them to be inspected as they develop, and dead or infertile eggs to be removed. Baskets are usually made to hold a maximum of 10,000 eggs in two layers, which is equivalent to the number laid by a 12 lb hen fish. The eggs from larger fish may have to be split between two hatchery

baskets, but where smaller fish are involved, it is not
advisable to mix their eggs to fill up the space available, as
this can lead to heavy losses if one batch is diseased or
infertile. Dead eggs are easily recognized as they turn white
due to the precipitation of proteins in the yolk, and if
nothing is done about them they are rapidly attacked by
fungi which may spread to healthy eggs nearby. In traditional
hatcheries, dead eggs are removed daily from the incubation
baskets either by picking them out individually with
forceps, sucking them into a glass tube connected to a
rubber bulb, or syphoning them into a bucket for disposal.
Once removed they should be treated with disinfectant and
either buried or disposed of away from the hatchery.

Daily egg picking is time consuming, tedious and expensive. A modern development in hatcheries has been to treat
all the incubating eggs daily with a fungicide, leaving dead
and infertile eggs mixed with live ones, and sorting them out
at the eyed stage when they can be handled without damage.
Malachite green is the preferred fungicide for hatchery use.
A stock solution is made by dissolving 2 oz in 10 gallons of
water (10 grams per litre). The flow through the hatchery
troughs is reduced to about 5 gallons per minute, then 3
fluid ounces (85 ml) of stock solution are added at the
inflow. As soon as the malachite green has been flushed out
of the trough, the flow is returned to normal. The strength
of solution, water flow and contact time are not critical, but
the treatment must be repeated daily until hatching is
complete if fungus is to be controlled. If the water goes on to
supply ponds containing older fish the treatment should not
be done at feeding time.

When the eggs reach the eyed stage they are 'shocked'
either by gentle mechanical agitation, or by syphoning them
into a bucket. In contrast to eyed eggs, those which failed to
fertilize are very delicate and are damaged by this process,
which causes the yolk membrane to rupture, turning the
eggs white. One or two days later the the dead eggs are
removed by hand picking, by floatation in weak brine in
which the eyed eggs sink, or by passing the whole batch
through an automatic sorting machine.

The elimination of the need to hand pick eggs daily has led

to the development of compact incubators in which they can be left undisturbed until ready for sale as eyed eggs, or until they hatch. Drip-feed incubators are the most economical in their water requirements, consisting of a cabinet containing a stack of trays holding the developing eggs. Water fed in at the top trickles through the eggs to the drain at the bottom, but there is no provision for holding alevins in the incubator, and eggs must be transferred to conventional troughs before they hatch.

In the vertical flow system, which uses more water, each tray in the stack consists of two compartments: a covered basket containing the eggs and a moulded dish in which it rests. Water is fed from above into the bottom of each dish in such a way that it flows upwards through the egg basket and overflows to the feed pipe leading to the tray below. Incubation systems are only possible if fungus diseases are controlled by chemical dosing (if malachite green is used, 3 fluid ounces of the stock solution are added daily to the top of each incubator). In open-flow systems the eggs should be treated daily, but in closed circuit systems using re-cycled water (which may be heated) chemical dosing may be necessary only once or twice a week, but the system has to be flushed with fresh water and refilled after each treatment.

Eyed eggs are very hardy if handled gently, and can be transported successfully in insulated containers if packed in ice. As a precaution against the spread of disease, it is usual to treat eggs both before shipment and on arrival, by immersing them in a dilute solution of a suitable disinfetant, but it must be remembered that this offers no protection against virus diseases transmitted inside the egg.

After hatching, the alevin wriggles out of the incubator basket and lies quietly on its side at the bottom of the trough, or incubator dish, until nearly all the yolk in the yolk sac has been absorbed. Both eggs and alevins are harmed by direct sunlight, so it is important that they should be shaded or kept in darkened hatcheries. When they start to feed they do so by sight and so require a low level of illumination such as is provided by diffused daylight. At this stage, alevins become active and are known as swim-up fry.

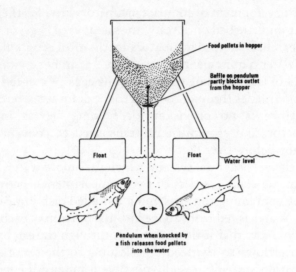

An automatic feeder

Traditionally they were weaned on minced raw liver which had been rubbed through a sieve to produce a cloud of small particles when added to the water, but fresh liver is difficult to prepare and keep, and has been replaced by dried powered foods in all except the smallest hatcheries.

Fry soon learn to eat, although mortalities may reach a peak at this stage, but the rule for feeding is 'little and often'. Labour costs can be reduced by using automatic feeders which dispense measured rations at regular intervals throughout the day and night, but these are an aid to the hatchery manager rather than a substitute for his skill and judgement, which are still required to ensure economical use of food and the optimum growth rate for the fish.

To avoid overcrowding, which can result in a reduced growth rate and avoidable mortalities, even when food and oxygen are plentiful, fry are moved at this stage into raceways or circular fry tanks.

Raceways are shallow linear ponds supplied with a strong flow of water to provide ample oxygen and to flush away waste products. Circular fry tanks may be from 6 to 15 feet in diameter, with a tangential inflow and central drain, which result in a self-cleaning spiral flow pattern. As the fish grow,

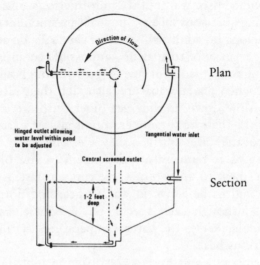

A circular fishpond

they are thinned and transferred to a succession of larger ponds and tanks until they are large enough for release.

Compared with brown trout reared from hatchery-bred parents, sea-trout in hatcheries have poor growth rates. Since both are grown side by side under identical conditions, this has been interpreted as evidence that the two strains are genetically distinct since it must be nature rather than nurture which accounts for the difference. Whilst this may be true, it is not evidence for sea trout being a separate species of fish. Hatchery trout have been selected over a number of generations for size and growth rate, but only the best are chosen as parents. In contrast, the vital statistics of sea trout taken from the wild for stripping are not known, but even though their offspring may have a lower growth rate than their cultivated cousins, it is probable that their genetic diversity gives them a better chance of survival in the wild than fish which have been selected to grow well under ideal conditions.

Age Determination and Scale Reading
The true facts of the life history of salmon or sea trout can only be established if it is possible to tell the age of

individual fish. Without this information we can only guess, making questions such as: 'how old are smolts at migration?', 'how long do adult fish spend in the sea?', 'do adults return more than once to spawn?', impossible to answer.

Unlike us, fish continue to grow throughout their lives, even when sexually mature, although their rate of growth may slow down as they get older. Fish are cold-blooded animals, their body temperature is almost exactly equal to that of the water in which they live. The rate of biochemical reactions is temperature dependant, a rise of 10°C may cause them to go two or three times as fast, so fish can be expected to be active in warm water and dormant in the cold, although each species is, of course, adapted to a particular range of water temperatures within which it functions best.

Temperate and arctic waters have an annual temperature cycle which follows the seasons, and which determines the availability of food and the rates at which fish can grow. Fortunately, the internal structure of the bony parts of fish varies with the growth rate, so that it is possible to recognize growth patterns which can be related to annual growing seasons. Things are much less convenient in tropical waters where steady temperatures may lead to continuous growth in warm-water fish, but the age of salmon, trout and other temperate species of fish can be determined by examining their skeletons. In cross section, round bones such as ribs or fin rays, show annual rings, rather like a tree. However, these are small structures which are difficult to read, even under the microscope. Flat bones increase their area faster than their thickness, so structures such as the gill cover or otolith (a small bony structure in the inner ear) may show annual growth zones when examined whole, but it is the bony scales in the fish's skin which provide the most convenient structures for the study of growth rates in salmonids, as these can be removed for examination without killing the fish.

Scales first appear as small outgrowths from the skin along the lateral line when fry are about one inch long, and rapidly spread over most of the body with the exception of the head, gill covers, fins and tail. Once developed, the

A section of skin-scale

number of scales on a fish remains constant throughout life, a number which, within defined limits, is characteristic of the species to which it belongs. Salmon have 120 to 130 scales along the lateral line, whereas sea trout have only 110 to 120.

Because their number is constant, scales must grow at the same rate as the rest of the fish if they are to continue to perform their function. If they grew slower than the fish they would leave it naked as it grew larger, if faster, they would stick out like spines on a porcupine.

Each scale consists of a hard plate of bone, similar to the dentine in our teeth, lying obliquely in a pocket in the dermis, the inner layer of the skin. The posterior edge of the scale projects beyond the dermis, overlapping the scales behind, and is covered by the epidermal layer of the skin. The upper surface of the bony part of the scale is covered in

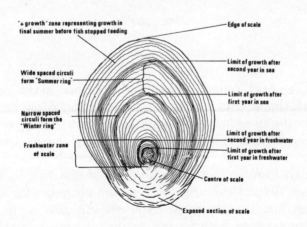

Fish scale showing growth rings

concentric ridges which form during growth as new material
is added to the outer edge of the scale.

These ridges can easily be seen using a hand lens or low
power microscope, but are not in themselves the structures
which are counted to determine the age of a fish. In summer,
when growth is rapid, the rings on the scale are widely
spaced, at periods of slow growth they are crowded together,
so if the scale of an older fish is examined it can be seen
to have concentric light and dark zones corresponding to its
growth pattern over the years. Lost scales are quickly
regenerated by the fish, but the record they carried is lost
for ever. Regenerated scales consist of a dense featureless
bony plate which shows structured growth only when it
reaches the same size as the normal scales around it. Such
scales are of no use for age or growth rate determinations.

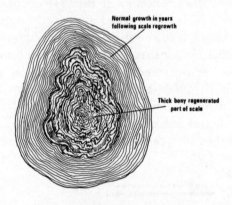

Regenerated scale

The growth rate of salmon and trout parr in the river is
much slower than that of adults in the sea, as can be seen
from the structure of the adult scale which consists of two
distinct areas. The inner part, around the nucleus, is
small and consists of narrow rings showing summer and
winter zones representing the life of the fish in fresh
water. Beyond this area the rings are coarser, with wider
zones indicating a much faster growth rate in the sea.
Non-migratory brown trout do not, of course, have sea-
growth zones on their scales, which resemble parr scales in

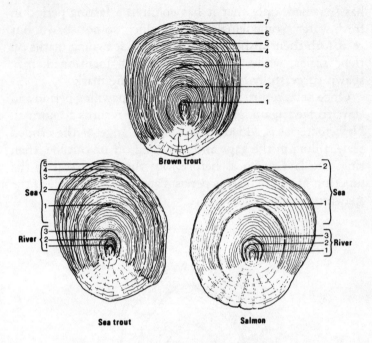

Comparative scales of Brown Trout, Sea Trout and
Salmon

their structure, except that they are larger and may have
many more annual bands.

The scales of salmon or sea trout which survive spawning
and return to the sea, may bear a spawning mark which is
seen as a discontinuity in the outer growth rings where scale
material has been re-absorbed by the fish at a period of
physiological stress when fasting in fresh water. Erosion of
the scale starts at the shoulder, the junction of the buried
portion bearing rings and the exposed part where rings are
less obvious, and gradually spreads around the edges of the
anterior, buried part of the scale. Erosion is greatest in
spring fish, which spend longest in fresh water as adults
before spawning, and may be so extensive as to absorb most
of the scale, leaving only a triangle of bony material.
Summer and autumn fish are less affected and late-run
autumn fish may show no detectable spawning mark at all.
The existence of a spawning mark is not evidence that a fish

has spawned, only that it has endured a fasting period in fresh water. Some female salmon which do not spawn, but re-absorb their unshed eggs, may show spawning marks on their scales, whilst others, as has been mentioned, may spawn successfully but show no spawning mark.

Once kelts return to the sea after the spawning period and start to feed again, growth of the scale returns to normal. New material is added to the uneven edge of the eroded scale, filling in the gaps and rounding off its outline, then rings are laid down as before, but the jagged scar at the junction of the two areas persists and is recognizable as the spawning mark in later years.

Spawning marks on a salmon scale

As the length of as individual scale is a nearly constant proportion of the body length of the fish, the ratio of the radius of an annual mark compared with that of the scale as a whole must be the same as the ratio of the length of the fish when the mark was laid down, to its length when the scale was taken.

The existence of this proportionality between the growth the growth of scales and that of the fish as a whole enables the history of length and growth rate for individual fish to be estimated without having to kill them by reading and measuring their scales. If necessary, the fish can be released

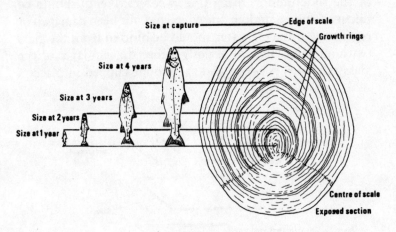

Fish growth scale

and further scales taken at a later date and it is not surprising that scale reading has become an important tool in the study of fish populations.

How to Read Fish Scales

Scales are best read using a microscope, but acceptable results can be obtained by mounting them in glass 35mm photographic slide mounts, projecting their images onto a screen and measuring them with a ruler. Scales should be scraped lightly from the shoulder of the fish anterior to the dorsal fin, above the lateral line.

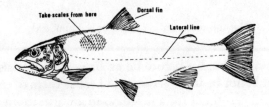

Location of scale removal points

They should be rubbed between the fingers to remove the pocket of skin, and transferred wet to one of the glass plates of the slide mount, using fine tweezers. Plenty should be taken to ensure finding one which has not been damaged or regenerated. Excess water should be blotted from the glass (without removing the scales!) before the top layer of the glass sandwich is added and the mount clipped in place.

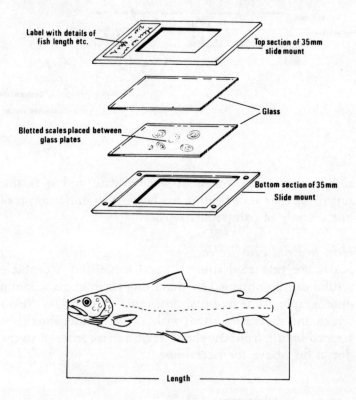

Method of mounting scales on a 35mm slide

Scales must be dry before being projected, but artificial heat should not be used as this could cause them to crack. It is best to keep them for a few days in a warm room to dry naturally before examining them. It is useful to practise with scales from a fishmonger's waste.

Assuming that scale length is proportional to fish size throughout life, the length of the fish Ln at age n is given by the formula:—

$$Ln = \frac{Rn\ L}{R_L}$$

where Rn = the radius of the annual band on the scale at year n,
L = the length of the fish when the scale was taken
R_L = the radius of the edge of the scale.

The use of this formula ignores the fact that fry may be one or two inches long before laying down any scales, and may result in an under-estimate of the size of a salmon when it was a smolt. Lee's formula is somtimes used to allow for this and is as follows:—

$$Ln = C + \frac{RN\ (L-C)}{R_L}$$

where C is the estimated length at which scales first appeared, and all other symbols are the same as before. C may be estimated as about $1\frac{1}{2}$ inches (38mm) for salmon and 1 inch (25mm) for sea trout.

Many other corrections have been proposed for estimating growth rates from scales, but these frequently rest on untried assumptions, or result in estimates whose accuracy is unjustified in view of the large errors inherent in measuring scales. Lee's formula is sufficiently near the truth for most applications, and where comparative, rather than absolute values are required, simple proportionality is adequate to describe growth rates.

Hatchery Stocking Policy

The risks to wild salmon and sea trout at large in rivers are so great that it is doubtful if more than 3 per cent of those which hatch survive their first year, and it is the vastly better success rate of hatcheries which makes them attractive as a means of augmenting the natural smolt-run of a river. However, a hatchery must decide at what age it can most economically release its product into the world. Parr are expensive to feed and house, so they should not be sheltered in the hatchery any longer than necessary. It is generally agreed that stocking with artificially stripped and fertilized eggs, or with newly-hatched fry, is unsatisfactory because the hatching rate of wild eggs in the redd is probably as high as 98 per cent so nothing would be gained by this practice. Stocking with fry is little more than an expensive way of feeding salmon to predators.

At the other extreme, it is frequently argued that salmon and sea trout should be planted into the river as smolts immediately prior to their migration out to sea. It is accepted that such a pratice does not appear to prevent them learning the characteristics of their adopted river, but the poor creatures have been used to regular meals in a comfortable fish farm, and to subject them for the first time to life in the raw when they are undergoing the stress of smolting is very unfair. In addition to the biological problems, stocking with smolts has economic disadvantages which make it only a second-best buy. The capacity of most hatcheries is limited by water supply, pond area, manpower or finance, allowing only a fixed quantity of fish to be held at any one time. Fish breed once a year and so hatcheries are managed on annual cycle. Fish kept longer than twelve months are not only consuming expensive food, but are taking up space that could otherwise be occupied by a larger number of younger, smaller fish.

If parr could be stocked into rivers as yearlings, the full potential of a hatchery could be used to produce the maximum number of parr. But can yearlings survive in the wild? At this age they have surmounted the crises of hatching and metamorphosis, they have the winter behind them, and some will soon be feeling the urge to migrate. On balance, this is the best time to plant out young salmon and sea trout, but they can be helped on their way if nursery streams are first cleared of predators. Also, competition with wild parr is avoided if hatcheries stock only those streams which are inaccessible to adult salmon and sea trout due to the presence of impassable waterfalls or other barriers to upstream migration. Stocking with yearlings not only gives parr a good chance of adapting themselves to life in the wild in favourable surroundings, but also more than doubles the capacity of the hatchery to produce fish, since the space they would have occupied in their second year can now be made available for extra fingerlings.

The planting of hatchery-bred salmon parr or smolts into rivers is an act of faith, hope and charity: faith in the ability of the fish to survive to become adults, hope that they will return, and charity in that the person investing in the fish farm does not normally expect to benefit directly from the increased salmon run he hopes to promote. Of course, altruism is not all. Most salmon or sea trout hatcheries are run by electricity-generating concerns to compensate for areas of spawning streams inundated by hydro-electric reservoirs, or for the loss of smolts due to fish being sucked into the cooling water systems of estuarine power stations. At least one hatchery is operated by a Scottish Fisheries Board to maintain the run in a commercially-fished river, and several more are run by English and Welsh water authorities in response to their duty to maintain, improve and develop freshwater fisheries.

Parr in the River
Scale reading has shown that amongst any group of fish of the same age there is a wide variation in individual growth rates. This is true both in the wild and in the more uniform conditions in hatcheries, where the availability of food and space are not limiting factors. This suggests that growth rate is controlled genetically rather than by the environment. Wild populations of salmon parr are known to contain both a fast-growing and a slow-growing component, but if growth rate is genetically controlled, how has this situation arisen? In a population of animals subject to the pressures of life in the wild, a stable genetic characteristic can only persist if it confers an advantage on the individual, or is important in securing the survival of the species as a whole. So at first sight it appears to be contradictory that both fast and slow growth rates should be of advantage to young salmon. It would appear that big is not always beautiful.

The advantages of a high growth rate are self-evident. It enables a fish to compete successfully with its fellows for food and territory and to reach the critical size for migrating as a smolt as soon as possible. Having smolted younger it will return as an adult younger than others, having been exposed to fewer dangers. Fast-growing fish could be expected to have a better than average chance of survival, and to be most likely to become the parents of the next generation, that is if the advantage of a fast growth rate to the species as a whole was as great as it would appear to be.

The advantages of a slow growth rate are less easy to see. Indeed, slow growing fish appear to be disadvantaged as individuals, and yet the genes conferring this disability persist in the population. If 'slow growth rate' is not to be eliminated, in spite of being a handicap to individual fish, it must persist by being of advantage to the species as a whole. Slow growing parr will smolt later, spending one or two years longer than the others in fresh water, and it seems that this is the reason why such fish are useful to the species. By having both slow- and fast-growing young, the salmon ensures that the offspring from any one year's spawning remain in their parent river for a number of years and contribute to a number of smolt runs. If one year's smolt run is exterminated by a natural disaster, or another year's spawning is unsuccessful, there will still be parr in the river to migrate out to sea the following spring. By paying the premium of short-term disadvantage to individual fish associated with a slow growth rate in fresh water, the species as a whole has been able to insure against natural disasters leading it to extinction.

Smolting and Migration out to Sea
When a salmon parr reaches a length of between 5 and $6\frac{1}{2}$ inches it is ready to undergo the physiological changes which will enable it to migrate out to sea as a smolt the following spring. The age at which this takes place is determined by environmental factors, such as water temperature and food supply, as well as by the fish's inherent growth rate. In productive rivers with a long-growing season, such as the Dorset Frome, Hampshire Avon and Test, as many as 90 per cent of salmon parr are ready to change into smolts as yearlings, in the spring following that in which they hatched. In cooler or less productive rivers things take longer. Only a few yearlings migrate in the Welsh Dee where 90 per cent of

smolts are two years old and a few spend three years in fresh
water. In Northern Scotland over 60 per cent of salmon
smolts are three years old, and in northern Scandinavia, at
the limit of the range of the species, they may spend as long
as seven or eight years in fresh water.

When they leave their home river, salmon and sea trout
smolts face many unfamiliar problems connected with life in
the sea. The two environments are so different that
relatively few species of fish are able to cope with both. In
British waters, only flounders, mullet, sticklebacks, smelts,
salmon and sea trout are able to cross the estuarine barrier which exists for other species, because the saltiness
of sea water and the purity of fresh water make diametrically
opposite physiogical demands on them. In most cases,
adaptation to one environment precludes life in the other.

A fish swimming in the sea consists of a dilute solution of
salts and organic molecules separated from the saltier
outside world by the cell membranes at the surface of the
skin. For life to continue, it must be possible for oxygen,
water and food substances to be able to get in, and for waste
products to be excreted. The membrane cannot be completely impervious, but it must be able to stop large
molecules escaping, or life would just leak away into the sea.
Where strong and weak solutions are separted by a semi-
permeable membrane, such as that at the cell surface,
water will flow from the weak to the strong until both
solutions are of equal strength. In the case of the sea fish, if
this was to happen the fish would lose water and would
shrivel up and die when its internal fluids became too
concentrated for life to continue. A similar effect can be seen
if a fresh grape is left overnight in a glass of brine. Sea fish
overcome this problem by drinking large quantities of sea
water. Their guts are able to absorb water whilst rejecting
most of the salt, and excess salts which do penetrate inside
the fish are excreted either via the kidneys or the gills. All
these processes consume energy, but are part of the price the
fish pays for staying alive.

The situation in fresh water is exactly the reverse of that
in the sea. Here, it is the fluids inside the fish which are more
concentrated than the surrounding medium, so that water

tends to flow in, and salts to leak out. If unable to cope with the situation a fish would absorb water until its body fluids became too dilute to support life, its internal pressure prevented any more water from entering, or it burst. Freshwater fish survive by constantly pumping water out of their bodies via their kidneys, which are able to sift out vital molecules and prevent their loss, but only by the expenditure of energy.

Smolts migrate seawards in May, June or July, but can be detected in the river as early as March. They congregate in shoals which feed voraciously as they move downstream. In slow-moving water they swim towards the sea, but where the current is faster they turn to face upstream and drift down tail first in the surface layers of the water. Pacific salmon smolts have been found to be active day and night, to prefer fast water and face upstream; active downstream swimming only occurs when water temperatures are high, and they are thought to migrate by drifting downstream with the current at night when they are less able to keep station in the river. By contrast, Atlantic salmon migrate by both day and night.

The changes seen in salmon and sea trout parr as they turn into smolts are an outward reflection of the internal physiological changes they are undergoing to adapt themselves for life in the sea.

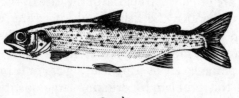

Smolt

The most obvious difference is that they change colour, losing their spots and parr marks under a silvery coating of guanine laid down in the upper layers of the skin. This process is controlled by the release of pituitary and thyroid hormones, and can be induced in parr by injecting them artificially with similar hormones extracted from the glands of cattle. The triggers which set off the change in nature appear to be increasing day length, light intensity and higher water temperatures. The process certainly has nothing to do with the onset of sexual maturity. Female salmon do not ripen until they return to fresh water as adults, and although some male parr become sexually mature in the spawning season preceding their migration, their testes are dormant by the time they start to change into smolts.

There appears to be a minimum length of about five inches below which parr are unable to become smolts. Fast growing fish may migrate when fifteen months old, but others which are below the critical size in the spring will have to wait another year or more until they are large enough to do likewise.

Poised between one way of life and another, smolts are very sensitive to stress. Many workers have experimented with salmon to see how rapidly, and at what age they are able able to withstand the change from fresh to salt water. Huntsman and Hoar subjected different sized salmon parr to various concentrations of sea water, and found that all died in mixtures containing more than three parts of sea water to one of fresh, but survived in solutions more dilute than one-third strength sea water, a concentration of salts similar to that in their blood. The higher the salinity the shorter the survival time, and the larger the parr the longer they survived.

Huntsman concluded that the increased resistance of larger parr was not due to a lower sensitivity of their tissues to sea water, but to the fact that as an animal grows larger, the ratio of its surface area to its volume decreases, and it takes proportionately longer for enough salts to diffuse through the skin to upset the parr's internal chemistry.

Jones carried out an interesting series of experiments when he kept smolts from the lower reaches of the Welsh Dee in freshwater tanks to which sea water was added at different rates. In every case where smolts were transferred directly into sea water they become sluggish after an hour or so, and lay passively on the bottom of the tank until they died. In one experiment, the flow of sea water was turned off and replaced by fresh water when the fish became torpid, and they were able to recover in about $5\frac{1}{2}$ hours. He found that, provided the change from fresh to salt water took longer than 10 hours, the smolts survived.

The conditions in large estuaries must make it easy for salmon smolts to linger over their transition from fresh to salt water, but this cannot be the case where mountain torrents run straight into the sea. Even so, there must be boundary layers where the salt and fresh water mix, enabling smolts to become acclimatized, for many such rivers support notable salmon and sea trout runs.

Fish Tagging

For as long as salmon parr, smolts and the adult fish have been recognized as belonging to one species, there has been speculation as to what happens to them between leaving fresh water and returning from the sea to spawn. Scale reading has established that maturing salmon spend one, two or three years at sea, but two overriding questions remain. Where do all the salmon go, and are the returning adults in fact the same fish that left their parent river as smolts? These questions can only be investigated if it is possible to mark individual fish so that they can be recognized at a later date, either when returning to their home stream, or at some distant place in the sea. The ideal mark should identify individual fish, be easy to apply, be readily distinguished by an untrained observer, should not harm the fish, alter its behaviour or impair its chances of survival in the wild. These criteria are mutually exclusive, and the marking method chosen must be at best be a compromise. Any mark which is easily distinguished is likely to make a fish more visible to its predators: a mark which identifies an individual fish will take longer to apply than a batch mark; any mark whatsoever must alter the fish's chances of survival in the wild.

The simplest way to mark a salmon or sea trout is to remove the adipose fin, or to clip or remove one of the bony fins.

In the latter case, it is usually the pelvic fins which are used as these are small and their loss causes least impairment to the fish. Bony fins are regenerated by fish, but the replacement is never the same shape as the original, and the line of the fin clip can frequently be seen as a boundary between the original and regenerated tissue. Fin clipping can only be used to identify batches of fish, detection of the mark in returning adult salmon and sea trout requires that all fish caught should be examined closely by trained observers, and the damage caused to the fish must lessen their chance of survival, if only by a small part of a

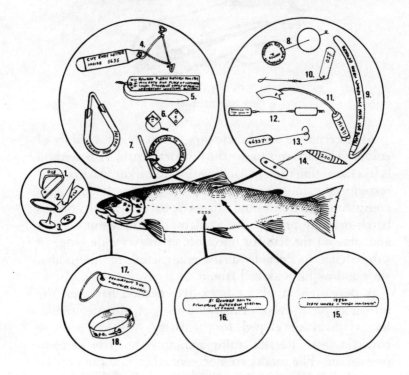

The main types of tags and their attachment sites:

1 strap	7 spaghetti	13 Sphyrion
2 plastic arrow	8 Petersen disc	14 roll and
3 batchelor	9 barb and trailer	anchor
button	10 spring anchor	15 subscutane-
4 hydrostatic	11 dart and	ous
(Lea)	capsule	16 body cavity
5 plastic flag	12 Carlin	17 jaw tag
6 ivorine/silver		pennant
plate		18 jaw

percentage. After marking, fish are usually treated with a fungicide such as Malachite green, and held for a few days before being counted and released.

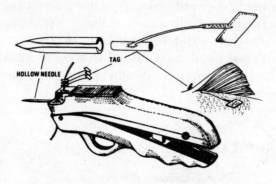

Floy tagging machine

An alternative to fin clipping is to inject a blob of coloured liquid latex under the skin of the fish. This method is less damaging than mutilating fins, but if the mark is to be recognized it must be visible and must make the fish more conspicuous than it would otherwise have been. Although a batch-marking process, the availability of different colours and sites on the fish for injection, enables a wide range of sub-batches to be individually recognized, the method is slow and requires skilled labour to apply.

A development of the latex-dye method has been the introduction of dye-spot marking using pneumatic, needle-less syringes developed for dentistry, which blast dye particles into the skin using a minute quantity of com-pressed air. The marks are not very large, and can only be applied where there are no scales on the body of the fish. The dyes used fade over a period of years, but the method is easy to operate and does not damage the fish. The use of differing combinations of colour spots and marking sites enables batches of fish to be distinguished.

In recent years, freeze-branding has become a popular method of batch marking as it is easy to apply, quick and kind to the fish. The branding iron consists of a copper beaker encased in insulating material, with one or more

copper tubes leading through to the outside. The outer ends
of the tubes are plugged, leaving a recess into which are
fitted the branding heads. These consist of short lengths of
brass rod with a letter, number or symbol standing up at the
end like a type-face. After fitting the branding heads into the
ends of the copper arms, the copper beaker is filled with
liquid nitrogen at a temperature of $-196°C$. Fish to be
marked are anaesthetized to prevent them struggling and
damaging themselves, and then held briefly against the
branding head. Without breaking the skin of the fish, the
extreme cold destroys the nervous control of the pigment
cells, which expand, and the mark is seen as a black figure
against the pale background. Freeze-branding marks grow
with the fish, but fade with age, although they are said to be
recognizable for more than two years. A team of four can
freeze brand 2,000 fish an hour. Freeze branding requires the
use of a special vaccuum flask to store liquid nitrogen, which
is not cheap, but damage to the fish is minimal and the
method has much in its favour. Similar techniques are used
for branding cattle, and in medicine for the removal of
warts.

A new, and as yet experimental, method of marking fish is
the use of a high-pressure spray-gun to embed minute
particles of fluourescent resin under the skin of fish, and is
advantageous in that fish need not be immobilized or
anaesthetized. They can be marked in bulk whilst being held
in a landing net and the marks are invisible unless viewed
under ultra-violet light. As a practical method for recogniz-
ing fish away from the marking site it can only be used if
specialist equipment is available. When used to assess the
return of smolts to their home river, all the adult run must
be caught and examined, but where such conditions do exist
it promises to be very useful.

Many problems in fishery management can only be
investigated if it is possible to identify individual fish over a
period of years, and this can only be done by fixing a
numbered tag onto the fish's body. The tag most commonly
used on salmon consists of a small piece of silver or plastic
about $\frac{1}{4}$-inch square, engraved with a number, fixed below
the dorsal fin by two strands of silver wire passing through

the back muscles and secured on the other side of the body. Other types of numbered tag may be fixed to the gill cover or the jaw of the fish. Although salmon are usually anaesthetized before being tagged in this way, the method does involve damaging the fish, it is slow and expensive and can result in the immediate death of up to 20 per cent of the fish marked. Mortalities on this scale should clearly be avoided and fish should only be marked as part of a properly designed and controlled experiment.

The Parent Stream Theory

The 'parent stream theory', that salmon return as adults to the river they left as smolts, was first investigated scientific-ally on the River Tay in Scotland in 1905, when some 6,500 salmon smolts were marked by threading a loop of German-silver wire through the flesh in front of the dorsal fin. No marked fish were recaptured that year, but in 1906, 42 marked salmon with an average weight of $6\frac{1}{2}$ lbs, were caught in the Tay, having spent just under a year in the sea. The following year, 57 marked salmon were taken in the Tay and in 1908, 9 marked fish with an average weight of $19\frac{3}{4}$ lbs were taken from the river. No futher marked salmon were caught in the Tay, but 3 marked sea trout were caught in 1909, showing that some of the smolts originally tagged must have been sea trout and not salmon. In all, 111 marked salmon were recovered from the River Tay, a recovery rate of 1.7 per cent, and a few were reported from other rivers.

These results support the theory that salmon return to their parent streams, but are not conclusive as a number of questions remain unanswered. Did all the tags inserted in smolts stay in place or were some lost? Did tagged smolts have the same chance of survival as unmarked fish? Was the behaviour of the two groups the same? Were all the marked fish returning to the Tay or to other rivers recognized by anglers and reported to the investigators? How many marked fish were neither caught nor seen?

Similar experiments under more controlled conditions have been carried out on several of the Pacific salmon species, notably the sockeye salmon of Cultus Lake in the Fraser River system. The outlet from the lake was screened so that all fish leaving or entering could be examined and counted. In the springs of 1927 and 1928 a proportion of the smolts were marked by fin clipping, and were expected to return to spawn one, two or three years later. Some did return and there were no reports of marked fish being caught in other streams, but it was found that the proportion of marked fish returning, 1.34 per cent, was less than half the 3.2 per cent found for unmarked fish of the same age.

In 1930 and 1931 the experiment was repeated, but all the smolts leaving the lake were marked. Of 365,265 smolts marked in 1931, 3,160 (0.87 per cent) returned as adults to Cultus Lake and 9,572 (2.62 per cent) were caught in commercial fisheries before they could return. Thus 3.49 per cent of the marked fish were accounted for, and none had been recaptured from other streams, confirming the parent stream theory. However, what happened to the fish which did not return? The earlier experiment, in which only part of the smolt run was marked, had shown that marked fish had only half as great a chance of returning as unmarked smolts and other evidence indicated that this was due to increased mortality following marking, but if this is taken into account in the 1931 figures, the corrected number of fish which should have returned to Cultus Lake is still only 7 per cent of those which were marked.

Three-quarters of these fish were caught commercially, and it is possible that tags may have been missed at the canneries. But even if this possibility is allowed for, it seems unlikely that more than 10 per cent of sockeye salmon leaving Cultus Lake as smolts actually return from the sea. These results are not inconsistent with the parent stream theory, but mean that the theory should be put in its proper context. It must be accepted that the great bulk of salmon migrating out to sea as smolts do *not* return to their parent stream, but of those which do return to fresh water the majority return to the stream of their birth, although a few may stray into other waters.

Support for the parent stream theory was obtained by Went, using Atlantic salmon in Ireland. Instead of marking smolts he tagged kelts, that is adult fish which have just finished spawning, on the basis that 10 per cent of these fish could be expected to spawn a second time. Returns of tagged fish were low, only 794 out of 33,682, indicating that tagging mortality must have been high (over 3,000 were expected to return), but of 724 fish recaptured in fresh water, 718 (99 per cent) were taken from the same river as that in which they were tagged.

Further evidence for the parent stream theory comes from the results of transplantation experiments where salmon species have been introduced to waters outside their natural range. Not all have succeeded, probably due to climatic differences between the donor and recipient river systems, but where salmon runs have been established, for instance the chinook salmon in New Zealand, their behaviour has been consistent with the parent stream theory.

Acceptance of the parent stream theory not only answers questions, but poses new ones. If salmon return perferentially to their native river, how do they get there and how do they recognize it, having arrived? Before attempting to explain how these questions might be answered, we must first consider whereabouts in the sea salmon have to return from.

Life in the Sea

Immature salmon are not found in estuaries after the smolts have run, nor are they caught in British coastal waters, although the intensity of fishing effort for other species is such that they could be expected to be caught accidentally if they were there. The only sea fisheries for salmon around the British Isles are for returning adult fish, and tagging experiments have shown that these were destined to enter fresh water very shortly, had they not been caught by the nets. The situation in Britain is not reflected over the whole of the salmon's range. Immature fish are frequently caught in the Baltic, although in some cases they have been found up to 600 miles from their point of release, whereas in the Bay of Fundy off Nova Scotia, netting experiments have shown that many salmon do not move more than fifty miles from their native rivers.

It has been suggested that, where large rivers are concerned, salmon may be able to recognize a 'zone of influence' and may not stray very far, but that smaller rivers are unable to maintain such a zone in the sea and salmon from these waters wander further away. If this is the case, European salmon rivers must be considered in the 'smaller' category.

Tagging experiments on returning adult salmon in Scottish waters have shown that fish marked off the eastern coast do not have far to travel before entering a river, but that those found in north-western coastal waters travel considerable distances to the south or east before entering fresh water. Menzies concluded that the feeding grounds from which these fish are returning must be to the west of Great Britain and Norway. Support for this theory was obtained when European and Canadian tagged salmon were caught on the West Greenland banks in the early 1960s. Salmon had first been reported in this area in 1883. It was fished by French trawlers in 1930, and catches of salmon from West Greenland increased throughout the thirties, but the area really came into prominence as a fishery in the sixties, the catch increasing from 55 metric tons in 1960 to over 1,000 metric tons four years later, a figure only slightly below the total salmon catch by rods and nets in England, Scotland and Wales. Tagging experiments have now established that salmon from British rivers can be found at West Greenland, and that fish marked there return to our waters.

But is West Greenland the only sea-feeding area for our Atlantic salmon? This fishery may only have been exploiting the fringe of an ocean-dwelling population of salmon extending out into the Atlantic, or it may be the only one of a number of feeding grounds to have been discovered. Until more is known on these points it is impossible to assess the true importance of the Greenland fishery in relation to the survival of the Atlantic salmon as a species.

Migration and Navigation at Sea
It is now accepted that salmon can distinguish their home stream, do return to it in preference to all others and travel many hundreds of miles from feeding grounds in the sea before finding their way home, but the question is, how is it done? The fish starting from Greenland, heading for a

British river, is faced with two problems. First, which way should it go, and then, how does it know it has arrived? As long ago as 1880 Frank Buckland suggested that salmon may recognize their home river by its smell, and recent work suggests that he was almost certainly right.

It is known that eels have a sense of smell which is as acute as that of a dog, and sharks have been observed following the trail of a prey fish which had swum out of sight. Minnows have been trained to discriminate between the natural odours of different freshwater streams, and have been shown to remember the information for several days. Could salmon have similar powers? They would need to be able to recognize the smell of their native river and remember it throughout their time at sea. If this was possible it would explain how they recognized their parent stream. In one experiment to test this theory, mature coho salmon migrating up the Issaguah river on the Pacific coast of America, were caught from adjacent tributaries, marked and returned to the river downstream of the point at which it divided, after half the number of fish had been prevented from detecting odours in the water by having their nasal openings plugged with cotton wool.

The great majority of normal fish returned to the tributary they had chosen on their first run, but those with cotton wool plugs returned to both tributaries in a nearly random fashion, as would be expected if it was smell which was attracting them. But what is the attracting substance, and can its odour be remembered over a long period? In 1934 it was suggested that salmon in the sea might be able to detect the smell of salmon parr in the outflow from a river, although this theory was put forward to explain salmon missing their way rather than being an explanation of the homing mechanism.

It has recently been shown that it might indeed be the smell of parr which attracts salmon to their home stream, and work to test the theory is continuing. In the late 1950s the Somerset River Board stocked the headwaters of the River Tone with salmon eggs. The estuary of the river disharges to the Bristol Channel and supports a small commercial salmon fishery. Following the planting, the catch of adult salmon rose significantly for a few years, only to fall again when planting ceased and no more parr remained in the river. Some of the fish caught had been tagged as smolts on the River Usk on the other side of the Bristol Channel, so although these findings suggest that more salmon were attracted into the Somerset river whilst parr were present in the headwaters, it does not prove that they return only to the river of their birth.

Evidence for a specific homing response was produced by Sutterlin and Gray, two Canadian workers who monitored the return of wild and hatchery-reared Atlantic salmon in a river which had been dammed as part of a hydro-electric scheme. Fish traps were built at the dam and at the hatchery, 1,500 metres downstream. 97 per cent of the wild fish swam past the hatchery and were caught at the dam, only 3 per cent being caught at the hatchery trap. More significantly, 67 per cent of the hatchery-reared fish were caught in the hatchery trap despite the fact that the hatchery discharge contributed only 0.1 per cent of the river's flow. Tank tests showed a clear preference amongst hatchery-reared fish for diluted hatchery effluent rather than river water. Wild fish showed no preference either way and both groups avoided well water, which was a component of the hatchery flow. This shows that it is not flow alone which attracts salmon up a river and that pure water from underground does not contain the attractive substance.

If it is indeed the smell of parr, remembered from their youth, which attracts salmon into rivers, at what dilution can it be detected, and how far out to sea does it spread? Maybe this is the factor which determines the 'zone of influence' around the estuaries of large rivers, but the odour of the River Itchen cannot be expected to extend to Greenland. How do salmon manage to navigate vast distances by dead reckoning? Faced with this problem we can only make guesses of what may be, based on a knowledge of the abilities of the fish.

Tagging experiments have proved that Atlantic salmon move too fast in the sea for the migration home to be the result of passive drift in ocean currents, but this does not prove that they know which way to swim to get home in time for the spawning season. Work on Pacific salmon suggests that the percentage of fish returning to fresh water could be accounted for if fish set out from the feeding grounds in random directions and swam straight on until they reached coastal waters they recognized or were literally 'lost at sea'. If this theory is unacceptable we must suppose that salmon are able to navigate actively from place to place in the sea. This implies that they must know where their goal lies in relation to their position at the start of the journey and be able to swim in the right direction for up to 2,000 miles without getting lost. It is interesting to speculate how this might be achieved.

The most useful clues to a salmon maintaining direction over a prolonged distance are light, gravity, water currents, electric and magnetic fields, all of which are themselves directional. Light in the sea comes from the sky, which is perceived as a circular 'window' at the surface, frosted by the turbulence of waves. Salmon at a depth of 50 metres would not be able to see the stars, but they should be able to determine the direction and altitude of the sun to within 6° of arc, provided the sun is shining. Laboratory experiments have shown that fish can be trained to orientate to the sun, and it is possible that salmon could use this 'sun compass' reaction as a navigational aid in the ocean.

Fish can only detect currents if they can see or feel a fixed reference point. When placed in a water current they usually head upstream, but find themselves unable to do so if they cannot see or feel the bottom. Fish held in tanks in static water, but with a moving background, will swim to keep pace with it, blinded fish in flowing water drift with the current. The threshold current speed for these reactions is a flow of 2.5cm per second (0.04–0.1mph), which is within the range found on the continental shelf where fish might swim within sight of the bottom, and currents could be the clue for migration in shallow seas. In deeper water fish are likely to be out of touch with the bottom, but where surface currents are moving with respect to the underlying water, it might be possible for fish to detect this movement at the boundary between layers by observing the apparent motion of suspended particles on the other side of the boundary.

It has been suggested that fish in the oceans, away from landmarks, may have an inertial navigation system, using the specialized structures of the inner ear to detect gravitational and acceleration forces, but the forces associated with normal swimming speeds and oceanic currents are too small to make this a probability.

Any electrical conductor moved through a magnetic field induces an electrical current at right angles to the field and the direction of movement, and this is the basis of two possible navigational systems for fish. An ocean current in the northern hemisphere, with a speed of 1 knot, flowing through a magnetic field of 0.4 gauss will induce a voltage of 0.2 microvolts per cm across the body of moving water and this could be used by fish to detect the current. On the other hand, the fish itself is an electrical conductor and will induce a voltage across its body when swimming in a magnetic field. If such a voltage could be detected it could form the basis of a navigational system, but neither this, nor any of the possible mechanisms for long-range navigation already mentioned has yet been shown to be the one which salmon actually use.

Compared with salmon, the problems faced by sea trout searching for their spawning rivers are insignificant. Evidence from tagging experiments shows that they are far less specific than salmon in their need to return to their parent stream. If they find a suitable river at the right time, they swim up it. Furthermore, it would appear that the feeding-grounds of sea trout are not far from the coast, and may be within the zone of influence of local rivers. Many sea trout are caught in coastal waters on the south and east coasts of England, but sea trout are seldom found further out to sea. Much work remains to be done on the detail of the life of sea trout, which are less important, economically, than salmon. Until more is known about their movements, their life at sea can only be described in generalities.

Upstream Migration in Fresh Water

Anglers are well aware that salmon runs differ between rivers. One may be noted for its large 'spring' fish, another may attract a high proportion of grilse, which have spent only one winter in the sea, or may receive the bulk of its incoming fish in the autumn. Are these inherited characteristics, or are they a reflection of the environment to which the fish have been exposed? Are fish in a river similar because it attracts only a certain type of fish, because only a certain type is available to be attracted or because the characteristics of that type are passed from generation to generation? With the wide variety of stream conditions encountered by salmon in fresh water, and the fact that those which do return to spawn tend to run up their parent river in preference to all others, it is not surprising that local races of salmon have developed, genetically different from those in other rivers. In the Pacific basin this process has run to completion, with the evolution of separate species of migratory salmonids which exploit different parts of the freshwater environment.

In the case of the Atlantic salmon, which constitutes a single species throughout its range, fish from different rivers are still sufficiently similar to be able to interbreed, but it is becoming increasingly apparent that the population in each river has evolved inherited factors to match local conditions. The existence of such a mechanism would account for the many failures which have resulted from attempts to re-establish salmon runs on rivers recovering from pollution, or where artificial barriers had been fitted with fish passes. Wherever possible, artificial stocking should be done with fish whose parents came from the river itself, and for this reason it is important that steps should be taken to conserve the salmon stocks of individual rivers before they are extinguished, when the last salmon has gone it may be too late to retrieve the situation.

The existence of genetic strains of salmon suited to their own river conditions would also explain the failure to induce spring runs in summer-fish rivers by re-stocking with fish from spring-run rivers. It seems that the time salmon spend at sea and the season they return to fresh water are controlled by a fine balance of genetic and environmental factors which may be unique to each river system.

With abstraction and impoundment becoming increasingly important in the management of water resources, a great deal of attention has been focussed on the problem of identifying which stimuli induce salmon and sea trout to run from the estuary into the river, so that the effects of river management on fisheries can be minimized. It is part of the folk-lore of fishing that salmon run up rivers in response to freshets or floods, and this is certainly so when there are obstructions which can only be negotiated in high water, but fish-counts at the head of the tide show that salmon enter rivers under all flow conditions, although at periods of high and moderate flow they arrive in greater numbers than they do when flows are low or extremely high.

What would salmon and sea trout do if the extremes of river flow were eliminated? Most of the rivers frequented by salmon are mountain streams where the ratio of the highest and lowest daily flows over the year may be as great as 200 : 1; however, salmon are also found in the chalk streams of southern England, where the ratio between high and low flows is about 6 : 1 and sudden freshets do not occur because most of the flow of the river is derived from chalk springs. Under these circumstances it has been found that the number of salmon and sea trout moving upstream reaches a peak in June, July and August, and again in October-November-December. Daily variations in the number of fish moving seem to be unrelated to river flow or water temperature. There is some evidence that larger fish move earlier in the year, but this tendency is not marked, and most fish move either during the night or when the water is turbid. Under the stable flow conditions of chalk streams, the basic pattern of salmon migration appears to be regulated by season, whilst changes in temperature, flow and light intensity play only a secondary role. In rivers where flows are more variable, flow becomes a dominant factor influencing the upstream migration of salmon and sea trout, but as the season progresses, smaller flows have a greater influence on the runs of fish.

The past fifty years have seen an explosion in our knowledge of the habits and requirements of salmon and sea trout. Anglers' tales have been confirmed or discredited, but each new discovery makes us more aware of the gaps in our knowledge. Perhaps this is how things should be.

CHAPTER THREE

The River as a Habitat for Salmon and Sea Trout

Gilbert Hartley, BSc, MIBiol, DipRMS, FZS

Four factors are involved in a productive game-fish river. There must be suitable gravel for spawning, a flow of clean water, an adequate food supply and the river must be accessible from the sea. Some of these factors vary in importance during the season, but lack of any one imposes a ceiling on the productivity.

The last and first feature, where the life story begins and ends, is the nature and extent of the spawning ground. Salmon and sea trout spawn in gravel banks of individual quality. Traditionally, salmon are said to use gravels with stones of fist size, while sea trout favour a finer grade which might be described as nut-sized. In fact, in Scotland the salmon use the coarse material, but in England there are many rivers where such material is uncommon, and the salmon breed freely in finer grades of gravel; there seems to be a local habituation to local conditions, not perhaps surprising in a fish restricting itself to one ancestral environment.

The gravel of spawning grounds is worked by the hen fish as a preliminary to egg-laying; she washes it into a hollow by tail-movements, and after spawning covers the eggs, which are retained in the hollow by eddies, with more gravel from upstream. It is therefore essential that the gravel should be free to be worked, and not compacted into a solid mass by infilling with clay or ferruginous material.

Occasionally, suitable banks of gravel can be brought into use by mechanically disrupting the hard covering of a compacted bed, but this needs caution; streams and their beds grow in sympathy, and by weakening what amounts to

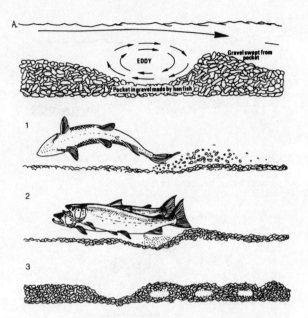

Redd cutting and spawning. A. ova and milt is
trapped by eddy in pocket cut in gravel by the hen
fish. 1 Hen fish washes the pocket in the gravel.
2 The fish spawn. 3 The eggs are covered as the
fish move upstream, repeating the process until
spent.

a groyne, the distribution of flow, and hence the existing
pattern of gravel banks, may be unsettled.

In stable conditions, river gravel banks migrate slowly
either up or down stream as the years pass, though a severe
flood may scour them away and some years elapse before a
quasi-stable system reappears. As a rule, salmon ova are
buried sufficiently deeply to survive normal spates, which
do not alter the bed topography, and for the eggs to be moist
when spawning has taken place in a spate over an area
subsequently left uncovered by water; the chief hazard in
these circumstances is a long frost. Normally the water will
be up again in time for the hatched alevins to move around.

It was shown by the late Dr T. A. Stuart over twenty years
ago, that salmon and sea trout select suitable spawning areas
on the basis of water currents rising from the gravel.

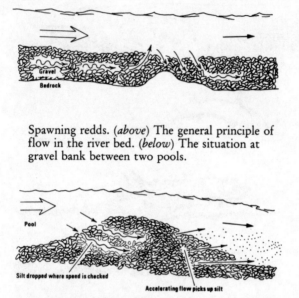

Spawning redds. (*above*) The general principle of flow in the river bed. (*below*) The situation at gravel bank between two pools.

A river may be considered as consisting of water flowing in the hollow of the channel, and more water flowing around this in the interstices of the stones of the bed. Where a rock outcrop occurs, the water in the interstices is ponded and can only flow by emerging into the channel, and where the bed dips downhill, or a hump exists in the bed, and the flow accelerates, water is drawn down into the gravel upstream of the dip and flows out again on the downstream side.

This results in a filtration of the ground water, which drops its silt where it is checked by flowing slowly among the stones, and picks up loose silt as it emerges. Ova laid where there is an up-current will therefore be kept clean and free from silting. Dr Stuart observed that when examining sites, the hen fish spread out their pectoral fins on the gravel surface, as though investigating vertical currents, and sited their redds accordingly. A completed redd would itself form a hump, silting up on the upstream side and providing filtered water for the entombed eggs, with means for the alevins to reach the surface in due course.

It is therefore possible for suitable spawning sites to exist

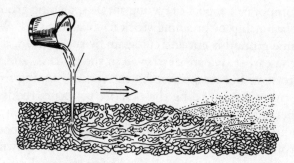

Use of funnel and pipe to wash out a suitable
gravel bank before pouring ova into it.

even in muddy rivers, though there is a greater risk of disaster
than in clear water, and on the whole, the artificial planting
of ova in them would be better done by using a Kashmir box
than Vibert boxes buried in gravel banks. The ideal must
always be, of course, to let the fish get on with their own
business; work put into extending possible natural spawning ground is always to be preferred to taking substitute
measures.

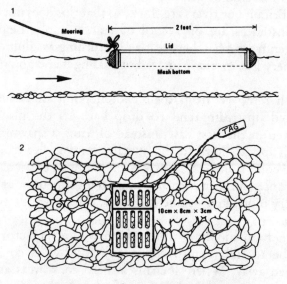

1 Kashmir box floated on the water surface.
2 Vibert box buried in an artificial redd.

An important aspect of having ample spawning ground is the relationship of breeding stock to available area. Where the same ground is cut and cut again by successive waves of fish, the earlier ova are destroyed in the process, and these tend to have been deposited by the earlier-running fish. In some rivers it used to be the practice to secure redds with wire-netting as the fish left them, to protect them from subsequent excavation; in Canada wholesale electrocution of surplus stock has been used to protect early spawnings.

In the less-favoured British conditions the surplus fish can be trapped and stripped, the ova being put into artificial redds in inaccessible streams, from which the fry can drop down, or they can be hatched artificially and distributed. What is not permissible is to hatch the ova in a spring-fed hatchery, and then distribute them as un-fed fry in an ice-bound river.

In the long rivers of America it proved to be the case that the salmon were very accurately adapted to the distance to be covered both downstream to the sea and back to the spawning ground, and failure to recognize this wrecked the original large-scale hatchery operations, as both smolts and adults matured at inappropriate times.

In Britain our rivers are short, so that this does not occur, but instances are on record of reared smolts being dis-charged from a hatchery leat and returning as adults to the hatchery leat *en masse* instead of passing it and going on up river.

Fish removed from their chosen point in a river and planted upstream tend to drop back to the place they selected in the first case, instead of using a spawning area which appears ideal to the human observer. Sea trout, not being conditioned to a single river, might be expected to be less conservative in their reactions, but the behaviour would be very individual—some fish stray, others definitely come home

The food supply of fish in rivers is rarely a factor which can be usefully improved, as any additive is constantly flushed away. Where lochans in hard rock areas are con-cerned, the stunted local stock of trout can be improved by fertilizing the water, and the dumping of cut bracken into field drains has been used to provide for a supply of water-fleas downstream. In the same way, the use of chalk debris tipped into streams which are normally acid has had beneficial effects in raising the pH value and thus relieving the fish of the physiological burden of counteracting disadvantageous conditions, so that they grow better. The modern problem with all activies of this kind is the cost of carrying them out, and the identification of the best investment.

The timing of the food supply plays an important part where salmon are concerned, and a rather less part with sea trout. Alevins given the opportunity to feed before the yolk-sac is absorbed start their free life bigger than alevins left unfed until all their yolk has been absorbed; many of these last never acquire the trick of eating at all—it seems to be a revelation bestowed on some alevins but denied to vast number.

In the natural course, an open winter will result in earlier hatching and an earlier food supply, and a severe winter will retard both. In comparison with Scotland, most of the English salmon rivers have a climatic advantage which results in a longer growing season, as the fish have an earlier start.

This is extremely important, as the productivity of a river depends, in the last resort, on the number of first-year parr it can feed. From the initial situation where a myriad of tiny mouths are scouring the stones for minute prey, starvation and predators change the pattern to one where a few far larger mouths are competing for a far wider variety of tit-bits—and these include any available small fish. These casualties do not, however, represent a loss to the system as a whole; they have played a valuable part in concentrating into an available form, food otherwise inaccessible to the larger fish.

At the same time, it is reasonable to have this concentration done as far as possible by species not capable of constructive survival.

Ideally, one would rear ova in streams freed from competing species and isolated by obstructions; at the end of the first summer, the parr would drop down into deeper water and a wider range of feeding before migrating in the spring. In pratice, the operational needs would result in disadvantages quite counterbalancing the theoretical advantage; it is better to accept the wasteful ways of nature which have, after all, maintained the stock hitherto, than to replace the whole untidy system by a logical artificial one which depends on human infallibility.

The essential point about feeding the first-year parr is that if the river can do this adequately, there will be no need to feed second-year parr, since the smolts will migrate early in their second spring, leaving the site vacant for their successors.

This results in a greater productivity in the river, and greater return size, as there is a loose inverse relationship between smolt age and age at maturity—grilse commonly have a two- or three-year smolt age, singles being very rare indeed, and the forty-pounders are generally maiden fish with a one-year smolt age.

Against this must be set the fact that grilse do not seem to stray into the areas where high-seas fisheries for salmon have been reported, and thus may be less at risk, though all share equally in the coastal fishing hazard off their native shores, which is a greater danger, and one with relatively selective action on specific rivers in the vicinity of netting area.

Sea trout, as distinct from salmon, take far more out of the river and bring far less back. Their smolt age is never less than two years, and frequently three; the smolts are often twice as large as salmon smolts, and the adults return in their first summer as whitling, finnock, or sewin, or in the next as the equivalent of grilse. Some of the finnock spawn, and from then on, annual spawning is the general rule; sea trout live longer than salmon, and a dozen spawning marks are sometimes detectable in the scales.

Maybe their longevity is made possible by their habit of feeding in the river before descending as kelts after spawning; sea trout kelts are quite difficult to identify even by scale-reading, and the amount of food needed to mend a thousand sea trout kelts in early spring is obviously a heavy tax on the river, and presumably on the newly-emerged fry and parr also.

Indeed, it is one of the unsolved puzzles of ecology that sea trout in a river do not not take it over completely from salmon, as they appear to be far better adapted to river life than their rivals, and both species occupy almost identical biological niches.

Sea trout appear to be physiologically adjusted to brackish water rather than neat sea water, in which they are more delicate than salmon, and die more readily, whereas the reverse is true for salmon. The Baltic sea trout reach weights of about fifty pounds in comparison to the salmon, which very rarely achieve twenty in that diluted environment.

The fourth factor, accessibility, is the limiting one without which the rest become irrelevant. It is also the one over which some constructive control can be exercised where necessary; where fish cannot ascend a river, it is possible to help them to do so. This help may be physical or legal, and it must be borne in mind that the desent of rivers, by migrating smolts, is even more important than the ascent by adults—it is the destruction of migrating smolts which kills a river off more certainly than severe attrition of migrating spawners.

British salmon inhabit short rivers, unlike the former European stock, and in consequence there is a minimum of distinction between the spawning areas of spring and summer fish, and only indistinct gaps in the sequence of entry from the sea.

We have to be prepared to accept salmon in any month of the year, and access is required at all times and not only

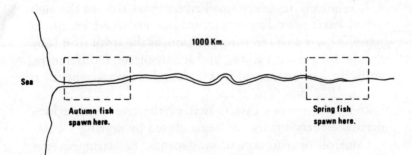

Notional distribution of salmon stock

during short and rigidly-defined periods of a few weeks during which the entire stock rushes upstream. Fish-pass design for Pacific rivers requires as much consideration of peak traffic densities as any underground railway system.

The development of hydro-electric power in Scotland has produced a situation where legal sanction has been given to the operation of fish-passes during certain months of the year only; this was originally intended to avoid wasting expensive water in periods when no fish had been known to require passage, but it has the effect of freezing the situation in a set pattern, failing to take account of seasonal peculiarities, and not allowing for the progressive changes of behaviour consequent on the change in environment. Following hydro-electric exploitation there is always a drop in the fish stock, but this is followed by a recovery as the local population adapts to the changed environment, and it would be wise to accomodate such a possible development.

Access to the river from the sea is, in its physical sense, a problem for the future, when water supply barrages produce terminal lagoons from which a token allocation to a fish pass represents the attraction intended to guide the fish, but a plausible solution will have to be avaible before design is undertaken; it is essential that the fishery advisers have an initial situation from which they can, if expedient, retire slightly in the light of experience, and not a sub-marginal situation from which advance is impossible. The deadliest weapon salmon conservators face is the *fait accompli* backed by statutary delays during which the stock becomes extinct, and with it their legal rights.

A relatively few very small rivers enter the sea through gravel bars, providing attraction but no access except in spate. This is an interesting position, as the small river is by nature a sea trout habitat, and sea trout run indifferently, either in low or normal flows, though salmon respond to floods. For practical purposes this situation can be forgotten; the serious case is that of the river with a long narrow estuary capable of being closed by netting.

Control of this situation depends on stringent net limitation orders and weekly close times, leading to acrimony between the commercial netsmen and the anglers, and an automatic antagonism over expedient restrictions intended to cover an unusually critical period—to secure the palliation of a dangerous abuse on one side, the other has to make an ostentatious but valueless concession. In fact, both sides depend on the same fish, but only one is in a position to kill the goose laying the golden eggs, and while the commercial and sport fisherman fight each other, interests with no concern for fisheries can exploit their mutual differences and destroy the environment for both sides— usually by removing the water.

Quite apart from the medieval interest in ensuring free passage for salmon, immortally laid down in one Scottish ordinance—a gap as wide 'as a swine of 3 yer elde, well fed, is of length so that neither the grouzie nor the tail may wyn till any side' (Calderwood 1909) the technicalities of the problem of getting fish past obstructions have been studied for more than a century, and an enormous quantity of information is available.

The accepted British practice is described in the Report of the Committee on Fish-Passes issued by the Institution of Civil Engineers in 1942. In the light of subsequent experience, minor modifications could be suggested to this, and the introduction of the Borland Fish-lift came after its publication.

Borland passes are, however, specialized structures for securing passage at high dams, and the recommendations given in the Report are safe, though passes with submerged orifices have not proved as overwhelmingly successful as was anticipated. Dr Pryce-Tannatt made fish-passes the subject of his Buckland Lectures, and these were issued as a book by Edward Arnold in 1938. There are also several authoritative reports by W. J. M. Menzies and by W. L. Calderwood, as well as a mass of academic studies. On this account, and for the reason that no-one could now instal a pass without the agreement of the local water authority, which is responsible for accepting the design, it is more profitable here to consider fish-passage in principle than in detail.

We may start from the premise that a migratory fish has an urge to travel up (or down) stream if it recognizes factors which encourage it to do so. Its progress is not automatic or inevitable, but is a response to stimuli which are not yet identifiable except in the broadest outline. Fish can therefore still surprise us by their behaviour, and we can make mistakes in designing structures for them.

The most important factor, which governs all fish movement, is that the fish is cold-blooded. This means that the rate at which it can bring its reserves of fat into action, and consume them, depends on the water temperature. Quite simply, a fish in cold water is not as powerful as it will be when the river has warmed up; apart from that, a big fish is stronger than a small one, and can attain a higher swimming speed.

Fish do not in fact swim very fast—about six lengths a second seems to be their limit. The impression of great speed is due to their almost instantaneous acceleration, but against this must be set the fact that they cannot sustain high speeds for many seconds, but rapidly become exhausted and have to rest. Failure to rest and re-balance their reserves, which are used fast but incompletely in emergency, results in a lethal accumulation of by-products; this is the usual fate of fish stocked into an already-populated stream, and cease-lessly harried by the entrenched inhabitants until they drift away downstream in a moribund condition.

On the other hand, when not operating under stress, salmon can cruise almost indefinitely; the height to be ascended at an obstruction is not significant, provided that the fish does not have to take it in one rush. An American experiment with Pacific salmon in an artificial pass, where they ascended from pool to pool on a kind of hydraulic treadmill, showed that they can climb thousands of feet without distress; the end only comes when the fuel runs out.

In terms of fish-pass design, this means that it is possible to hold fish back by installing a pass which requires sustained effort to ascend it. It is commonly said that salmon will not face white water till May; white water in a fish-pass means entrained bubbles, which absorb the available power of a swimming fish, which therefore works ineffectually, literally beating the air. To provide for this waste of energy it must burn more fuel, thus needing a reasonably high river temperature to make this possible.

The situation is different where the required effort is short. In a pass with overfalls connecting a series of pools, a fish can locate itself close to the fall and swim up it, or jump into the crest in a short spasm of activity which produces a completed result, and then rest if necessary.

The design of fish-passes has developed from an original concept of providing a gentler slope than the obstruction, and thus reducing the speed of flow; early passes conform to the type called 'rough channels' because the friction of their surfaces is enhanced by using blocks or baffles to cause turbulence. A rationalized form of this is the *Denil type of channel*, which has U-shaped baffles to create a counter-current. These pass fish successfully up a slope of 1 in 4, and

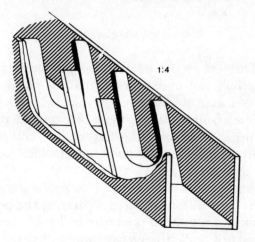

Denil channel

being standardized can be cheaply constructed, but must be interrupted by resting pools if the rise is more than 6 feet.

A convenient but uncertain variant of the rough channel pass is the *diagonal baulk*, once popular at weirs with a sloping back. In this case a dwarf wall is led obliquely from the toe of the weir to a notch in the crest, and provides a channel up which fish can swim. Diagonal baulks are unpopular with designers because, though they are cheap and often work to perfection, nobody has ever discovered why one baulk is a success and an identical one a complete

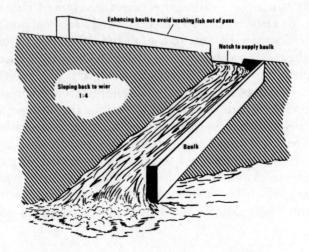

Diagonal baulk

failure. They can be put in as a quick gamble if expedient, but something less uncertain ought to be planned at the same time in case of failure.

All these channel passes might be expected to favour summer fish at the expense of springers, but whether this is a significant sanction depends on the geographical location of the site; some rivers are seldom very cold.

The most familiar type of pass is the *pool and traverse*, in which the water drops in steps separating the pools; the connection from pool to pool may be by an overfall or a submerged orifice. With overfalls, pool surfaces should not be more than 18 inches different in level, but with submerged orifices a difference of two feet is permissible.

It is probable that this very familiar type of pass is capable of considerable improvement in design, leading to the reduction of size and cost. The recommended dimensions for pools are 10 feet long and 4 deep, with a width of 6 feet, forming a large cistern. Fish are expected to swim from pool to pool, not jump. Dr T. A. Stuart, after a considerable study of the behaviour of fish at falls, recommended that the depth below the falling nappe should be just enough to allow the water to lose its energy without impinging on the bed, and that the pool should slope up to the tail like a natural

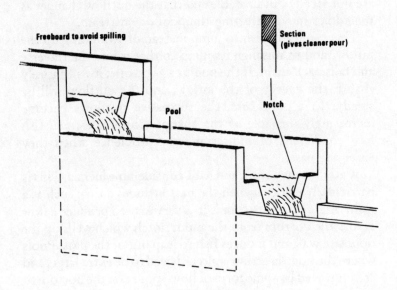

Pool and traverse pass

pool; in fact, a pool pass allowed to fill with gravel would automatically assume the best hydraulic shape.

This is an important consideration; fish working up a pool fish-pass have to assess the hydraulic conditions in each pool before attacking the inflow, and it is obvious in many cases where the pool length is minimal, that the conditions

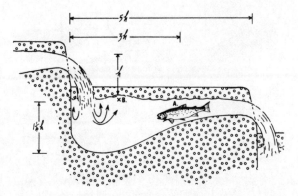

T. A. Stuart pool. Fish rest at (A) and jumps at (B).

are not steady but unstable and that the outflow changes as the eddies move, affecting the pool downstream.

This can lead a fish to jump instead of swimming up the inflow, and to misalign its jump so that it hits the traverse and falls back again. If the pool is a good one, it will entirely absorb the energy of the inflow, and the outflow will be steady. In a poor pass, the successive outflows become increasingly unstable as the energy accumulates, and fish face conditions of indiscriminate turbulence when they enter the pass.

Water is heavy stuff, and has a considerable inertia. This is particularly evident when the pass includes a turn such as a right-angle or dog-leg pool. It is very easy to produce a flow across the bottom from the input notch which wells up the opposite wall and induces fish to leap out of the pass. Pools where the flow direction is altered need to be extra large, and are improved by some form of flow-spoiler on the bottom to confine currents.

Spiral passes are particularly prone to turbulence; the water current flows at right angles from the notch in the radial traverse, and usually builds up into a transverse roller. Fish do not seem to take readily to this, possibly because they are disoriented. In any case, they are reluctant to traverse interfaces where there is shearing, and tend to avoid them by leaping.

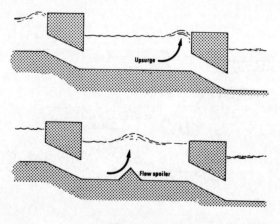

Flow spoiler

With any kind of fish-pass, the first and most important thing is to get the fish into it—after that everything is comparatively easy, but it must first be offered a path in which it can have some confidence. There is room for dispute between the advocates of a strong steady flow, and those who favour a good noisy outfall to advertise the entrance, and both schools can point to successes. These probably depend on the configuration of the pool or stream immediately downstream of the pass.

The usual difficulty facing the designer is a restricted flow of water with which it is difficult to make a convincing demonstration in face of the flow over the obstruction itself, but in ideal conditions the impassable flow can be used to lead the fish up to the entrance, and leave it facing a flow it can overcome.

The problem of leading fish into fish-passes is matched by the converse problem of keeping them out of mill leats or water intakes, either as smolts and kelts following the water flow downstream, or as fresh fish running up what promises to be the most important channel, but leads into a turbine discharge with no hope of passage further.

In principle, both hazards can be countered by providing impassable grids to prevent the fish leaving the river and entering the false channel, but the difficulty here is considerable. On the outlet, there is backing up of water to reduce the available head, and on the intake side, not only loss of head caused by the necessarily narrow bar spacing—3/8 inch is about the maximum to prevent smolt entry—but the effect on this of drifting debris.

An intake screen to be effective for its purpose must have a flow speed through it sufficiently low to allow smolts to swim away to safety. Higher speeds lock the fish onto the grid, where they drown, and very high speeds cause death by impact. A screen which is normally perfectly safe may be converted into a deathtrap by debris in a very few minutes, and large installations which depend on an unfailing water supply, such as power stations, instal complex automatic machinery for cleaning the screens. This may run constantly, or may be brought into action when there is a head differential across the grid.

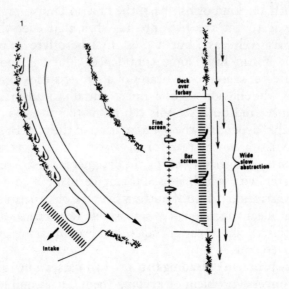

Screens. 1 How to trap smolts and debris. 2 Smolt-
free intake.

In fact, the protection of fish at intakes is a major
consideration at all installations, on account of the need to
protect machinery, the public relations aspect, the fabulous
cost of the exercise, and the damage to fisheries. The fish are
put last because the instinctive reaction of designers in the
past was to build a hatchery to make good the damage, but
in recent years better attitudes have prevailed, and constructive thought has been given to the avoidance of
producing a problem.

Generally speaking, an intake with a debris problem will
be likely to have a smolt problem also, and by adopting a
hydraulic design which minimizes the first, it is likely that
the latter can be made amenable to a simple electrical screen.

The basic rule is to ensure that the major flow is always
across the face of an intake, with a free escape route straight
downstream. This leads debris to drift past instead of
clogging the bars, and smolts are always reluctant to swim
through a bar screen of any spacing if they can avoid doing
so.

Naturally, industrial installations are the subject of very

careful design and discussion among the interested parties before being built, and should normally be safe enough, but misunderstandings occur, and fish behaviour may be wrongly assessed, or may be altered by the new works, so that vigilance is required at least until the absence of a real problem has been demonstrated.

One of the most destructive false-lead hazards existed formerly in the Avon and some other southern rivers where it was the pratice to 'drown' the adjacent meadows by means of a spread of small ditches which distributed the comparatively warm river water over the ground, the flow being controlled by sluices. Although the practice was not permitted in the smolt season, it was difficult to produce hard evidence of deliberate transgression, and vast numbers of the smolts, which begin to migrate as early as Christmas, ended on the ground as a prey either for birds or the drowner. Upstream migrants could meet a similar fate in a river where the correct course to follow was indeterminate.

The upstream hazard is the minor one; a fish blocked in one channel will eventually drop down again and try another—always provided that it had not been poached while waiting, and that an alternative is available. The classic locus has always been where a small river is used for milling, and the water flows either in the stream bed or in the mill lade, but not both, except in time of flood.

The law formerly recognized this state of affairs as inevitable during working hours, but required the sluices to be opened when milling was over for the day.

The legal extension of the term 'milling' to cover the generation of electricity resulted in an abuse by which it became possible to continue working throughout the entire 24 hours indefinitely, and thus to confine a head of fish downstream of a weir. Economic changes have now made it more expensive to maintain a private turbine than to use mains power for industrial uses, and water charges can be applied to the installation, so that this is one of the vanishing hazards where individual sites are concerned.

Large scale difficulties arise in the case of hydro-electric installations, where a very careful balance has to be struck between national requirements and local fishery interests.

The obvious cases of the South and the North of Scotland Hydro-electric Boards illustrate the lengths to which fish conservation can be carried in designing such enterprises. The fish-passes of the Galloway scheme, involving gigantic engineering works, with pools of the then latest design, have been modified over the years in the light of experience. The more recent Northern schemes have relied less on long flights of pools than on fish-lifts of the Borland type; these are simpler to construct but have to be designed perfectly in the first instance if they are to work at all, and rely on mechanical operation.

As has been pointed out earlier, in cases of river management there is no substitute for accurate information. Catch reports do not represent the number of fish available, and personal observation of fish movement is far from reliable.

One of the effects of the industrialization of salmon rivers has been to make it necessary to devise automatic fish-counters which provide information on the pattern of movement in response to variations in flow.

The use of human observers at suitable points is both fabulously expensive and unreliable, as the hypnotic effect of looking at nothing for hours on end results in hallucinations. Various types of mechanical counters have been described, but the modern system is to use either electrical or acoustic detectors.

This is not the place to describe the scientific bases of the many types theoretically possible; a few general observations on types which have been satisfactorily used is more relevant.

The basic point is that the counter must detect a fish and record its detection. It does not even have to be precisely accurate, though it has to be precisely consistent in its error. A counter which is steadily 50 per cent low in its record will show when fish move, and in what relative numbers but a counter which is exactly accurate except in some transient condition of flow or interference is useless; cases where a river with an annual count of some 150 salmon is suddenly invaded by 17958 during one night have the same effect as the clock striking thirteen—something not only absurd in itself, but casting doubt on everything already said.

There is no difficulty in obtaining signals from fish; the trouble arises in excluding spurious signals from other sources, and it is this which leads to complexity in design. Of the two major types, the electrical resistance bridge has the advantage in simplicity over the acoustic type except in odd situations where no ambiguity is possible. For instance, an echo appearing at the exit of a fish-pass and moving upstream can only be a fish, but an echo recorded on the back of a weir can be absolutely anything, and has to be analyzed to determine its plausibility.

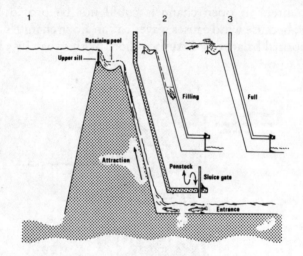

Borland pass. 1 Attraction stage. 2 Filling. 3 Full.

The original type of fish counter, developed by N. G. Lothlean for the North of Scotland Hydro-electric Board, was designed to count fish passing in each direction through a submerged tunnel of circular section, and to indicate by the signal strength whether they were large or small. The method is to balance the resistances in the tunnel between the centre and the two ends, and to detect the disturbance caused by the passage of a fish through both in turn. This only counts completed attempts to traverse the tunnel, and indicates the direction of travel and also the order of size of the fish. If desired, the recorded count can be validated by taking flash photographs of the fish at the instant of counting.

This is the most satisfactory method possible in the ideal conditions in which it was applied, but is limited. In some rivers, debris jams the tunnel; in others a special obstruction and tunnel have to be installed; in others there is insufficient depth for working. But the main drawback is that if the counter is intended to show the effect of variations in water flow or other factors on the movements of fish, the need for the fish to traverse a tunnel may easily bias the result and hide the effect required.

Counters in open channels could not be provided as easily, because wind causes waves to run along channels, and the normal balance is disturbed more by this than by a fish.

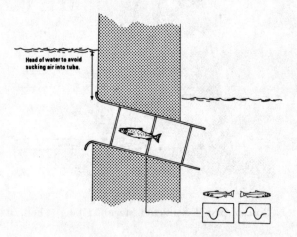

Electrode type of tube counter

The simplest situation exists at the Crump gauging weirs used for flow measurement. Here, on the back of the weir, the water surface is as smooth as glass, and by fixing three electrodes across it, two compartments can be formed. These are not equally deep, and as the water level rises their cross-sections change, and as the water conductivity alters with flow and temperature, this changes the balance of resitance between them. However, it has proved possible to produce an extremely reliable counter which will ignore these snares and produce an accurate count of fish down to a size of 8 inches, as long as the tail water level does not rise and lift the standing wave onto the lowest electrode, causing unsteady conditions.

A series of such counters installed at suitable weirs up a river can provide data on the time of entry and pattern of progress of migrant fish, with the proviso that in the lower reaches the count will be inflated by flounders and bass, and that the downstream count is never as accurate as the upstream, as there are more ways than one down a weir.

In order to separate the effects of recognized alterations of régime on the behaviour of migrating fish, it is therefore essential to avoid complicating their passages by introducing dubious obstacles; the simpler and more straightforward it can be made, the more obvious will be the effect of changes in flow pattern. Moreover, fish which are delayed are subject to predation and disease.

It may be worth considering the factors which control the behaviour of smolts, which combine the compulsion to explore unsuitable avenues for migration with a marked tendency to ignore seemingly obvious escape routes. They generally swim near the surface, though if penned back, they will dive 80 feet to exploit a chink in a smolt screen. Given an easy escape route, they will use it freely instead of entering a submerged intake or a surface intake which is not obviously passable.

Smolts use their eyes to a surprising extent, and can be manoeuvred by the use of visual signals. In many places they migrate mainly at night, and then avoid to some extent points where lamps cause a local change in the level of illumination; their eyes are good both in daylight and night time, but are slow to adapt from one condition to the other, so that an abrupt change in brightness is a deterrent to them. Where the stream drops over a ledge to form a fall, their behaviour depends on what they can see. If confident, they will go over the crest head first without hesitation, and as smolts are gregarious, one fish forms the first of an entire shoal. Where conditions are uncertain, a smolt hovers at the crest of the fall, head upstream, and makes tentative excursions before allowing itself to go—if it does. This spectacle is not lost on other smolts within sight.

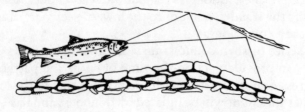

The fish uses the water as a periscope

The important factor for the smolt approaching the crest is what it can see at the bottom of the fall. At a smoothly rounded and level crest, the surface of the falling water seen from beneath as the fish approaches, forms a mirror in which it is possible to see a surprising amount; in the case of a Crump weir, with a 1:5 slope on the downstream side, an eye submerged to the level of the crest upstream of it can

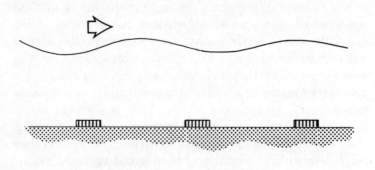

Waves in an open channel

examine the whole of the back of the weir. If the water flows into a pool downstream, the appearance is dark, but if the water falls onto rocks and is broken up, light is reflected up from the foot.

The fish approaching a fall thus has at least the chance of an advance warning of what lies ahead; if the view is favourable, it will go with confidence without hunting for something less dubious.

This behaviour can be exploited at smolt passes, where

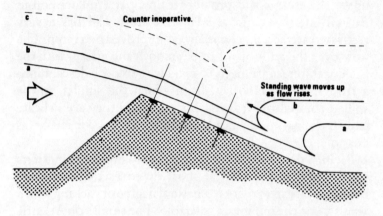

Counting electrodes on a Crump weir

the need is to lead the fish gently through a point of no-return into a contrived safe passage, in which progress is irreversibly downstream.

First, the smolt-pass must be located at a rational position, and appear plausible. Smolts swimming around a headpond looking for a way of escape will readily find a channel through the lip of a dam, or through the bank, but do not readily find the exit of an island Borland pass separated from the shore. As they are reluctant to pass between the bars of even a wide screen, if any alternative exists, the approach should be quite open.

It helps to clear smolts from a channel if the floor slopes

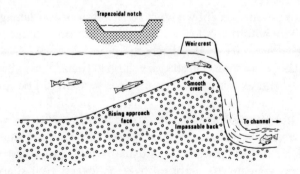

Smolt bypass

up to the escape; this provides a flow pattern common in natural circumstances; a step in a crest wall has a very restricted attraction, and is always improved by a ramp. The flow over the crest ought to be smooth and glassy, with the back of the crest arranged to produce a smooth descent into a trough, or other basin, from which the smolts can be spilled compulsorily; from this point on, they are delicate parcels being mechanically handled as expeditiously as possible.

Pacific salmon smolts are reluctant to enter a channel if its width requires the natural shoal diameter to be reduced below half its size; there is a natural degree of packing which seems to be the minimum tolerable. The smolts of Atlantic salmon are less exactly organized, but the same effect may exist. In experimental conditions, they used a by-pass 20 feet wide with great efficiency, but were impeded when the width was reduced to five.

As the scales of smolts are very loosely attached, it is necessary to protect them from abrasion; discharge down a long concrete slope in a thin layer of water is damaging, and in any case, predacious birds rapidly find where smolts are exposed in this way.

Common plastic drain pipes, which have a highly-polished inner surface, provide easily-assembled smolt delivery systems, and can be easily adapted to form electrical smolt counters. In certain American sites, smolts strained from intakes are transmitted down the dam in pipes at 6 ft/ per sec., and finally shot vertically upwards to fall freely into the tailwater.

Experiment has shown that vertical fall is not damaging, but there would seem to be risk of cavitation damage from negative pressure in the discharge pipe.

Atlantic salmon smolts are larger than many Pacific species, and extremely delicate. No effort should be spared to make their passage as uneventful as possible.

Although smolts often migrate in flood conditions, when the water is turbid, it does not follow that they are running blind. From underwater, it is usually quite possible to see objects against the light above, as every fly-fisherman knows, and submerged obstructions distort the surface around them. It is quite easy to make a smolt react to a non-existent fall by floating a suitable transparent wave-shape in its track. By the same token, it is highly probable that a fish will, when in the neighbourhood of an electrical screen, experience a visual flash as well as feeling the electric pulse. The flash, due to stimulation of the visual nerves, will not offer any picture—the fish is 'seeing stars', and at night this effect could influence its behaviour, though by day the interference with vision would be slight.

Controlling Fish with Electricity

The use of electrical fish screens has been mentioned several times in this chapter, and may be usefully considered in general terms, together with its limitations and advantages.

It is the converse of the more familiar electric fishing, or, rather, the converse of fishing with an ineffective set. An effective set forces fish to come to the positive electrode, and is designed to concentrate all the available voltage in a zone surrounding it, without producing excessive local fields which stun the fish. An ineffective set lacks the local

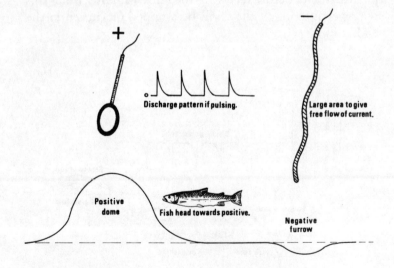

Electro-fishing showing volt drop and dome (a concentration of voltage drop at the positive electrode for collecting fish.)

power to force the fish to remain at the anode, and merely prevents them approaching the cathode. Normally as little power as possible is dissipated at the cathode, which need only be considered as an earth return—the electrical equivalent of the waste-pipe of a bath.

Electrical screening is a far more delicate operation, except in its simplest application; fish have to be induced to react as is intended, as there is seldom the chance to apply a coercive stimulus. Obviously, a fish swimming upstream will be brought to a halt if it is stunned, but a fish swimming downstream which, it is intended, shall be deflected from an intake, will inevitably be washed into it if in any way hampered in its movements.

The principle usually adopted both in upstream and downstream screens is to block the way with an electric field of increasing intensity, arranged so that the fish faces the cathode. This is an intolerable condition for a fish, which must turn to head in the other direction. Small fish, which occupy a shorter length along the electric field, experience a lower voltage difference between head and tail than large fish, and consequently can penetrate further into an augmenting field, before receiving the same stimulus, but if this is powerful enough they will be stopped or turned in the end.

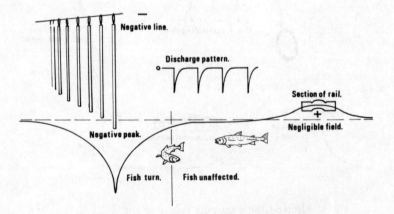

Electric field applied as a screen

The field is therefore arranged with large positive earth electrodes and behind these a line of small negative ones to produce an intense field, and these are usually supplied with pulses of direct current, because this produces the greatest effect with the least power consumption. The pulses are of the order of 10 or 20 per second, to ensure that an approaching fish experiences several and yet is not cramped. Fish trying to swim upstream are washed back by the water flow and do not remain in the field.

There have been many developments in fish screen design, one of the most important of which has been the use of electrodes connected diagonally to produce a vibrating field. While this is not essential for upstream screens, it is for downstream ones, as it prevents a fish drifting through backwards along a neutral axis. For preventing fish escaping upstream in small sites, where the cost of installation is high compared with the running cost, satisfactory results are obtained from the use of two rows of vertical electrodes spanning the stream, each row being connected together to form a common conductor, and the two supplied by a 24 volt transformer from the mains. Using accumulators to supply the more elaborate pulsing units is too onerous to be practical; there must be a mains supply or generating set.

It is not possible to give precise data, as the extent of the electric field depends greatly on the water conductivity and the nature of the bed, which often allow a result to be obtained by exploiting local conditions.

It is bad practice to use a screen as a simple blocking device where migratory fish are concerned; it should be used to make them take an alternative route avoiding the hazard which they would otherwise meet. This usually means installing the screen some way from the physical hazard, at a point where a reasonable choice of route exists. Most of the failures of electrical screens have been due to installation far too close to the hazard; a smolt caught in a body of water rushing towards an intake is in no position to obey a signal, however compelling.

The proper way to deal with water supply intakes is to ensure that the design provides for the inflow to be taken sideways from a flowing stream, so that debris floats past it.

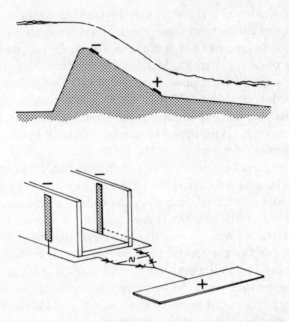

Split cathode screens to prevent fish running over a
sloping weir or up a leat.

An electric smolt screen then consists of a long line of
pendant iron pipes supported across the intake and extending some way upstream. These electrodes, about 1 inch in
diameter and 2 feet apart are connected alternately to make
two separate series, each serving alternately as the negative
electrode of a system in which the positive is a long rail laid
on the bottom parallel with the negatives and as far across
the stream as possible. Pulses at about 100 volts are applied
through a pulse-generator. Smolts swimming down close to
the bank upstream of the intake are taught by the unpleasant
tweaks coming from the negatives to keep clear of the bank
before they encounter the inflow, and are staved off until
safely past.

The important point here is that the water speed through
the screen—at right angles to the river flow—is slow, so that
the smolts can easily react against it. The fish are subjected
to a period during which they can learn how to avoid the
unpleasant sensation.

The practical limitations of electrical downstream screen-

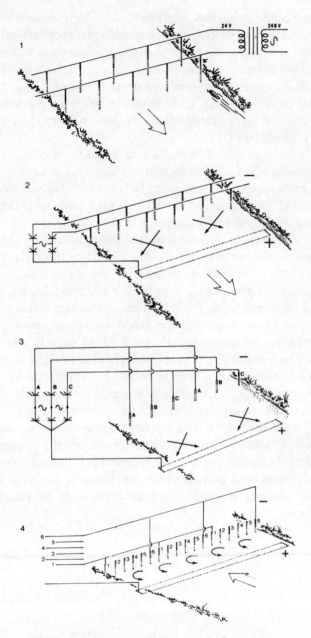

Various screens. 1 Simple AC screen (fixed field).
2 Split cathode screen with vibrating field (rectified
AC). 3 3-Phase screen using chopped DC (vibrating
field). 4 Sequentially pulse DC screen (travelling
field).

ing are obvious but not at all clear cut. Quite definitely the only certain way of keeping fish out of a place is to screen the water through a grid so fine that they cannot pass. Fish eggs and fry will enter—as they would through the best electrical screen—so that no system will prevent coarse fish getting into a trout reservoir. Even micro-strainers are no defence against ova regurgitated by ducks, which carry them past every installation.

Mechanical fine screens are a periodic nightmare to engineers, when conditions lead to a heavy trash burden, and this causes mortalities among the fish which the screens are intended to protect, as partial blockage leads to excessive flow speeds and impact damage on the screen.

In contrast, an electrical screen is unaffected by debris, which displaces the pendant tubes as it drifts through, and is free of the objection of obstructing the water flow.

There is a great deal yet to be learned about downstream electrical screens. At the same time, very exact tests carried out for years on end have failed to reveal any regular correlation between the efficiency of an electric screen—which may reach 90 per cent—and the electrical parameters; there is no sign of a critical point. However, the investigation would be economically rewarding; the whole thing comes back to an observation of smolt behaviour.

The real difficulty with electrical screen projects, except on a small scale, is that they are not unequivocally successful, so that the design engineer has to provide for a grid screen as a safeguard, and consequently the financial saving is lost, while the site is made disadvantageous for an electrical system.

CHAPTER FOUR

About Salmon Fishing

Conrad Voss Bark

Salmon fishing is a rare and much sought-after experience, partly because of the power and grandeur of the fish, and partly because of the incomparable beauty and wildness of nearly all the big salmon rivers. A man will travel a thousand miles to a remote wilderness, spend day after day on the river, and each day blank, yet go back the next morning full of an even greater expectation than before. The excitement when he feels the first heavy pull of a fish is beyond compare.

Even a moderately-sized fresh run salmon seems to have the power of a torpedo, and the run of a large one—a twenty-pounder or more—is an experience that will last a lifetime. There is, in addition, something great and majestic about the character of the Atlantic salmon—Salmo the Leaper—that captures the imagination. They have a strange glory as they come from the deep seas into the rivers on their spawning run, nor is fishing for them quite like any other fishing, for the salmon do not eat on their way to the mating grounds and if they are moved to take an angler's lure while they rest on their journey, no one knows what moves them to do so. They are a strangely unpredictable fish.

The full joy of salmon fishing can only come when you know your river, know where the rocks lie unseen under the surface turbulence of the water, and where the right place will be to put your fly so that it will sweep correctly at the right speed over the lie where the salmon rest after they have come into the pool. You must first go to a river with someone who knows these holding places, perhaps a gillie whose job in is to know, and he will point them out to you. This is important. You *must* know where salmon are likely to lie. Indeed it is so important that it should be written in letters of fire. It is the major of all major commandments.

Salmon are in general most inclined to take a lure when they have come fresh into a pool and the water is clearing—fining down as we say—after a freshet or spate. They are then active and there is an edge to their minds which makes them snap at something that crosses them. The longer they are in the pool the less inclined they seem to move to a lure, and the more they darken and lose their silver sheen and take on a pinkish tinge, and a potted fish, as we call them, is frequently untakeable. So, it is when salmon are fresh in the pools that it is best to go fishing, and the most pleasurable way of taking a salmon when conditions are right for it is on a fly.

The Fly Rod
The Americans use short rods, the British long ones, and both kinds will take salmon, so it is much a matter of habit and preference which type to use. Why so many like the long rod—the double-hander—is that it does have certain advantages in casting a longer distance, in keeping the back-cast clear of obstructions on the bank, in controlling both the fly as it goes over the lies and the fish after it is hooked. There is also a certain charm about a double-handed rod which is not easily defined, known as 'the feel', which is to do with its power and the feel of its power when playing a big fish. Those who do not like long rods say there is no need to have one to catch a salmon, which is true enough, and that a single-handed rod is much lighter and easier to use, which is also true, though whether it is easier to use does depend to some extent on the skill of the person who uses it.

A double-handed rod is of course heavier than a single-handed rod, but this does not necessarily mean it is more tiring, and the introduction of new materials—glass fibre and now carbon fibre, or graphite as it is called in America—has meant a dramatic saving in weight.

A carbon rod for double-handed fishing—12 ft to 14 ft long—weighs about 10 oz or so compared with 16 to 18 oz, for a cane rod. A carbon rod can throw lines of a casting weight that varies from No 5 to No 9—a tolerance no cane rod can achieve. It can, so it is said, throw the line further and faster, but this is disputed by some experts. No matter—it cannot throw the line any less of a distance so there is no handicap in that way on the debit side.

Carbon rods are so good—though still expensive—that many anglers believe they will eventually take the place of built cane and oust glass fibre as well. Maybe. Glass fibre is a wonderfully cheap material for the mass market. As for cane rods, many anglers and a number of dedicated craftsmen are determined to continue using and making them simply because of their quality. The feel and look of natural cane cannot be imitated by man-made fibres.

At the moment, therefore, we have an enormous selection of fly rods of all kinds, made in what seems to be the most remarkable choice of materials fishermen have ever had put before them. How our ancestors would envy us if only they knew. Even for my grandfather, salmon fishing was an arduous and physically exhausting business. He used a 16 ft rod of greenheart which would probably weigh between $1\frac{1}{2}$-$1\frac{3}{4}$ lbs, and *his* grandfather would have used an 18 ft rod that would weigh even more. To fish a big Scottish salmon river several hundred years ago was a very tough business.

Days long ago

In those days, rods were mostly homemade, 16 ft–18 ft long, with big butts of hickory wood, and the rod tapered to a flexible point of reed or cane. The early reels—they date back to the 16th century—were lashed to the butt with thongs. But as often as not the reel was a luxury. The casting line, of tapered horsehair, was merely attached to a loop at the top of the rod. There was no running line. If a very big fish was hooked, the rod and line were somtimes thrown into the river to try to avoid a break. The angler would follow the rod downstream and pick it up when the fish tired. He would be wet through and bitter cold. There were no rubber waders in those days. Mostly he would dangle a worm on the hook, but when the ground was too hard-frozen to dig a worm he would tie on a feather as a lure. A trailing feather was the beginning of the 'fly'.

No one really knows why a salmon lure is called a fly. It is not like a fly, not even a butterfly, though the long hackle feathers are called wings. Possibly the rod first used was the same rod used for fly fishing for trout where the artificial fly was an imitation of the natural. When the same fly rod was used for salmon it was still fly fishing even though the streamer feather was much more like a worm or an elver. It was the use of the rod that determined the name.

How our ancestors would envy us the choice of tackle in our shops. There are rows and rows of rods of all lengths and weights made from a wonderful variety of natural and synthetic materials, and designed for many different types of rivers. Which, of the many rods, do you need? Will one rod be enough, or two, or three?

For small salmon rivers that are no more than 5 to 10 yards across, and have a good many trees growing along their banks—well-bushed as we say—a single-handed trout or sea-trout rod of around 8 ft 6 in will be adequate.

For medium and large rivers one double-handed rod is usually adequate, at least to begin with—something around 12 to 13 ft long—that will handle both floating and sinking lines. If you are fishing a very big river like the Tweed regularly, in late winter or early spring when the water is very strong, then you may well need a 14- or 16-ft rod, but for most rivers a 12- or 13-ft rod is enough.

Should it be cane, glass fibre or carbon fibre? This is very much a personal choice. You can never get the 'feel' of a rod until you fish with it. Hire or borrow one if you can before you decide to buy. Try out several different types; carbon fibre (graphite) has great advantages but is costly; cane (bamboo) is very beautiful and has a wonderful action, but requires more maintenance; glass fibre is the cheapest and possibly the best buy if you do not fish very often. Try as many rods as you can before making a decision. Go to a good dealer, who will guarantee the rods he supplies against defects in workmanship, and buy the best you can afford. Very often the final choice is not too difficult; you will see and handle one particular rod that attracts you, and when you fall in love with a rod that is the one to buy.

Fly Lines
Look on the butt of your rod, just above the handle, and you will see a mark. For example, it may be No 9; that means the rod will work best with a No 9 line. It is absolutely essential that both rod and line are matched, if they are not, casting will suffer.

The flexing of the rod provides the energy which propels the line, and there is an ideal weight of line—the casting weight—for the particular springing power of each individual rod. If you use too heavy a line the rod will feel sluggish because the spring is over-loaded, and if you use a line which is too light it will not 'work' the spring of the rod and you will not cast very far.

Cane and glass fibre rods need a line that matches them exactly. Carbon (graphite) has a little more tolerance, and can work with lines of two or three different casting weights. A cane rod may only flex properly with a No 9 line whereas a carbon rod that works best with a No 9 can also work very well with an 8 or 10.

Lines are designed for almost every kind of fishing and water condition. Before the modern plastic line with its varying densities was developed, salmon anglers used a silk line which normally sank slowly unless it was greased to float. This is still the basic need, and so if you do not want to buy more than one line then it is best to buy a slow-sinking plastic line. A non-silicone grease can be used to make it float if needed, but make sure it is a non-silicone grease, otherwise the plastic coating of the line may be damaged. It will need greasing several times during a day's fishing, especially if there is scum on the water.

However, ideally you need two types of line—a sinker and a floater. A medium-sinker is probably the best for general use, but if you fish fast deep rivers you will certainly prefer a fast or very fast sinking line of high density. Avoid lead-cored and sinking-tip lines; the former are best suited to very deep reservoir or lake fishing from a boat, and although sink-tip lines may sometimes be of use in very fast rivers to prevent the fly skating over the surface of the water, the same effect can be obtained by using a yard or so of very heavy fast-sink nylon on the end of an ordinary floating line. Your basic equipment, therefore, is a line that sinks and another that floats.

Now we come to tapers. The diagram exaggerates them, but it serves to indicate the basic differences.

With tapers we come to an uncertain area where there is something to be said for and against all types. The most common line in use on double-handed rods is the double-taper, the DT line. It has advantages, one of which is that when one end of the line becomes worn by use, the line can be reversed and the other end used instead.

The forward taper or FT line has the great advantage that

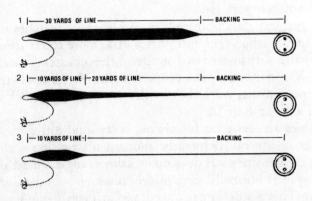

1 Double taper. 2 Forward taper. 3 Shooting head.

it can be cast further than a DT line. The casting weight is in the first 10 yards or so and the rest of the line is so thin it can be shot through the rod rings more easily than the thicker double-taper line. The long-belly line is a compromise between the FT and DT lines.

The shooting head is an extreme kind of FT line—10 yards of heavy casting line attached directly to monofilament backing and used only on single-handed rods for distance casting, especially on lakes and reservoirs.

The DT line is one which has the widest possible use and is also economical and pleasant and easy to handle when fishing. The FT line is not so economical, as only one end can be used, but gives greater distance. If you fish big rivers an FT line may be essential, otherwise the DT line is best.

The Reel
Always buy the best reel you can afford. Although a reel is only a storage place for a line, if a salmon is running and taking line and the reel jams—and it does happen—then you have lost your fish. Cheap reels can rust or get out of shape, and even good reels jam if they are not kept clean, free of sand or grit. Keep your reel well-oiled using the lubricant recommended by the manufacturer. In my opinion, the best reel is a perfectly simple un-geared reel, not a multiplier or an automatic. The more complex the mechanism the heavier it is and also the more likely it is to go wrong.

Always buy a reel with a spare spool, so that you have one spool with floating line on it, and the other with a sinker.

Salmon Flies
The Victorian-style salmon fly was almost purely decorative. It was a gorgeous confection of many colours containing feathers from rare tropical birds, beautiful to look at, delightful to fish with, but no more efficient in taking a fish than a single-coloured fly made from the end hairs of a stoat's tail. It used to be regarded as heresy to say so, but the pattern of fly is not very important. More inportant is size and tone—wherther the overall effect is light or dark. The choice of fly, therefore, is very much a matter of tactics and these we will discuss later.

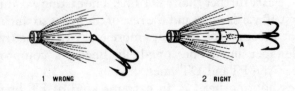

Tube fly showing correct hook position. A. Plastic
or rubber flexible tube to hold hook in place.

Hooks

We are concerned with four kinds, the traditional single, the
double; a long-shanked treble made up rather like a spinner
with the fly dressing on the shank; and the tube fly in which
the dressing is on a plastic or metal tube separate from the
treble hook. In the case of a tube fly make sure that the tube
is linked to the treble by flexible plastic or rubber tubing
otherwise the hooks will not lie straight.

The tube fly is very useful in heavy large sizes in fast
coloured water. In bright, clear, low water, a small single is
probably best. It is much a matter of personal choice. No
one has yet proved that a treble will hook a fish better than a
single, or indeed the other way round. Many anglers use
doubles as a kind of compromise. A deciding factor may well
be cost. Start with singles in the small and medium sizes, and
a few big heavy tube flies for thick and heavy water
condition.

Leaders

The leader can either be machine-tapered from butt to
point, or made up of various lengths of nylon knotted
together and tapering from, say, a butt of 20 lb breaking
strain to a point of 14 to 10. A typical knotted leader would
be a yard and a half of 20 lb nylon, a yard of 18 in the middle,
and a yard of 14 on the point. If the leader has to be tapered
more steeply, then the steep tapers come in the middle. The
length of the butt and point sections should not be reduced.
Tapering a leader is based on the same principle as the
whip—the smooth transmission of energy from a thick butt
to a fine point.

Most experienced salmon anglers make up their own

leaders; it is cheaper and they can use the tapers and lengths they like. In low water conditions in high summer a 12 ft leader on a floating line is by no means too long. With a sunk line in heavy water in spring the leader could be half that length. In low water in summer the leader point might be as fine as 7 lb breaking strain. In fast heavy water on the same river it might not be safe to go much below 16 or 14 lbs, and on a big Norwegian river the point might need to be at least 18 or 20 lbs. Take local advice, and if in doubt play safe.

Do not worry too much about getting the correct tapers on your leader, it is not so important as, for example, when dry fly fishing for trout, when, the tapers need to be quite precise to get a good turnover of a very light fly.

As the salmon fly is much heavier and the momentum greater, it will often go out nicely even when there is only one length of nylon between it and the line.

Knots

Unfortunately, many only discover the importance of this subject after losing a fish or two.

Learning to tie those knots which are necessary is a fairly easy task, but it is vital to realize from the start that only certain knots are suitable when using monofilament.

Usually there are several knots which can be employed for any particular task. Most anglers have their favourites; mine are as follows:—

For joining two lengths of nylon—the Blood.
For tying on the fly to the leader—the Tucked Turle.
For joining the leader to the line—either the Needle or the Nail knot.

The others that are useful to know are the Tucked Half Blood (which is illustrated in the section on Spinning) and the Blood Bight Loop which can link a leader to a line with the aid of a Stop knot, but if you have time to do them the Needle or Nail knots are safer and smoother for this purpose.

The following diagram explains, step by step, how to tie a knot which is continually used to make leaders and renew a point: the Blood knot.

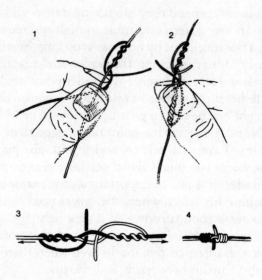

Stages in tying a blood knot

To make a really smoth join between the leader and line a
Needle or Nail knot are best. They are based on the same
principle, but the Needle knot is slightly more complicated.
A needle is pushed up the centre of the end of the plastic line
for about an $\frac{1}{8}$ to $\frac{1}{4}$ inch before coming out on one side.
Then the needle is heated slightly so that the line softens.

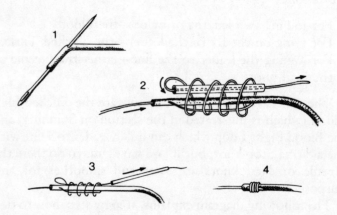

Stages in tying a needle knot

The needle is withdrawn and the butt of the leader inserted in its place. Next, hold a small diameter tube alongside the line and wrap the nylon round both the tube and the line, beginning at the far end of the tube and working back to the point of entry of the nylon.

When three or four turns of nylon are round both the tube and the line, put the nylon right through the tube. Hole the tube carefully so that the turns of nylon are not twisted, slowly withdraw the tube, and work the knot tight, pulling both ends of the nylon.

The Nail knot is tied in a similar way, but the plastic line is not pierced. The butt end of the nylon is merely laid alongside the line and tied as shown in the adjacent diagram.

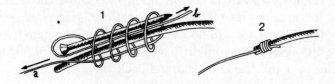

Nail knot. To complete the knot, withdraw nail
and tighten by pulling (a) and (b) with equal strain.

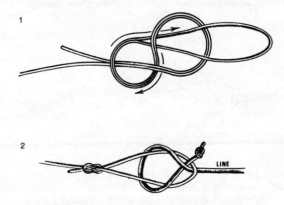

Stages in tying a blood bight and stop knot

However, it can be appreciated that the Nail knot does not produce such a smooth finish.

Glue can also bring about the desired result. Scuff the end of the line with a knife and use an epoxy resin glue to join the leader, and when dry, whip the whole joint.

The simplest join of all is a Blood Bight Loop and a Stop knot. The Loop is at the end of the nylon leaders which is doubled back on itself before the loop is made. Tie a simple granny knot at the end of the line and fix as shown in the adjacent diagram.

The best knot I have ever used for joining a salmon fly to the leader was shown to me by a well-known Spey fisherman and gillie, Hamish Menzies. It is a variant on the Turle knot, so as he had no name for it I called it the Tucked Turle. Place the nylon point through the eye of the hook. If it is an up-eye hook you put the point of the nylon upwards, if a down-eye hook downwards. Let the hook slide along the leader and forget about it while you tie an oridinary granny knot. A single granny knot will do for most small and medium flies, but a double granny might have to be used for a big fly in order to avoid the knot slipping back through the eye.

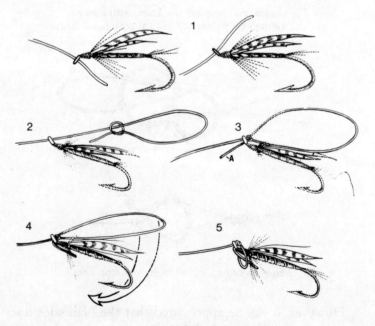

Tucked Turle

You will now have a running loop and a short end of nylon—marked A.

Bring the fly up to the loop and put the nylon end A through the eye of the hook.

Now turn the point A back under the hackle and bring the nylon loop down over the fly and draw it tight so that the loop traps the end of the nylon A against the underside of the eye of the hook.

It looks so simple that you do not think it will hold. But the tighter you pull, the tighter the loop presses on the eye of the hook and on the spare end of nylon A under the hackle.

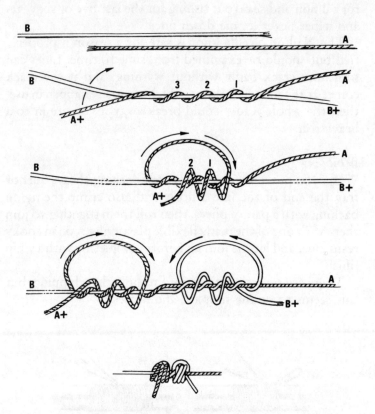

The Grinner. A new knot which is stronger than the Blood and easier to tie. The principle is to make three twists and then go back over them and make three more. It can be used to join line or tie hook.

So much for my choice of knots. There are many others but I know that these are reasonably easy to tie and will not pull out. The only knot that will sometimes let you down if you are not very careful is the Blood. Except when the nylon is very thick, when three or four turns will be enough, I now find that for real security you need at least five, six or even seven turns each side of the knot. And then after moistening the nylon, you have to slide the knot carefully so that it really is tight, and the turns sitting neatly together without overlapping. Well tied, the Blood knot will break before it will pull out.

The Tucked Turle is a superb knot and I have used it now for salmon and sea trout fishing for the last five or six years and it has never let me down once.

The Nail or Needle knot is safe for a season if properly tied but should be examined from time to time. Lines can somtimes crack badly without warning, and if the crack comes at the join of the knot, which can easily happen in use, then the whole leader could break away if you are in to a heavy fish.

Whipping

When you put a new line on to your backing always burr or fray the end of the line a little, and also crimp the nylon backing with a pair of pliers, then roll them together to join them with one of the many flexible plastic glues, or an epoxy resin glue, and let the join set before completing with a whip finish.

There are several methods of finishing the whipping, but this seems to be the simplest and neatest.

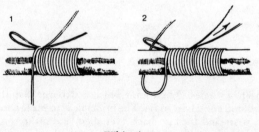

Whipping

Tie in a loop of nylon or thread, take several turns of the whipping over this loop and then take the whipping through the loop. Finish off by laying the end of the whipping through the loop, which is then used to draw the whipping line under the turns.

Nets and Tailers, etc.

You can load yourself up with a tailer, a net and a gaff or you can carry nothing at all. It depends partly on the river and partly on your likes and dislikes.

The safest way of landing a salmon is with a net. If you have a gillie the net will have a wide-gape—never less than 24 in—and a deep 'purse' long enough to hold a 40-pounder, and will be on a heavy wire frame on a fixed handle. If you are fishing alone you can still use a net of this type, carrying it from pool to pool and leaving it on the ground at the place where you would expect to net your fish.

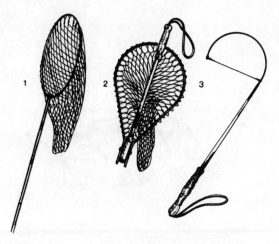

Landing nets and tailer. 1 Fixed net. 2 Carrying or 'gye' net. 3 Tailer ready for use.

Another kind of net, a smaller variety, is fitted to a sliding handle and carried in a sling over the back. My own personal preference is not to have anything on my back which might restrict movement.

A tailer is much easier to carry, but in practice it is not easy to use. The last time someone tried to tail a salmon for me the wire loop went over the salmon's head and broke the leader. I have not had an inclination to recommend the use of a tailer since.

A gaff, still used by some fishermen, can be hooked deeply into the body of the fish which is then dragged or lifted ashore. Sometimes anglers carry wading staffs with a gaff hook at one end. I am very much against gaffing, a practice which I find both cruel and unnecessary.

Salmon can be landed very easily without netting, tailing or gaffing, by what is called 'beaching' and this the method I normally use; but if I am going to a river where beaching is not possible, because—for example—of high rocky sides to a pool, then I use a long-pursed net on a fixed handle. The simplest equipment is the least liable to go wrong.

Using a 'priest'

One essential is, of course, a priest. This weighted stick is used to kill the salmon by hitting him on the head as soon as you have him secured in a safe place. He should not be left to die by suffocating in air. Hit him on the top of the head just behind the level of the eye. A priest is so-called—a grisly joke—because it delivers the last rites.

Wading Staffs

On big fast rivers where you wade deep, some kind of wading staff is a must! Indeed, almost the only time you will not need a staff is when you are fishing from the bank of a river you know has an even regular bed and a medium flow. Otherwise, take a staff. Avoid staffs with prongs at the top, those that float and those that do not have a rubber button at both ends.

When wading always have your back to the current. Take short side steps, sliding rather than lifting the foot. Use the staff in front of you as a third leg.

If you are pushed off balance and are carried away in the current, go downstream feet first—to avoid banging your head on a rock and to see where you are going—and above all don't panic. Keep afloat by paddling and you will eventually drift ashore, wet but alive! Crawl out and then look for

Wading technique. 1 The right way. The staff acts as a third leg and in an emergency can take your weight. 2 The wrong way. The body is easily unbalanced and the staff, held in one hand, cannot give full support.

your rod. After that look to your wallet, your watch and your whisky flask. I have known men carry on fishing, but it is best to go home and change.

Boxes and Bags

Some fishermen clutter themselves up with a mass of
equipment while they are by the river. I like to be as little
loaded as possible, wearing only a fishing waistcoat, plus a
padded jacket in cold weather. In the pockets I carry—a
priest, scissors, spare spools of nylon, fly box, and a spare
spool for the fly reel filled with the alternative line.

The fishing bag, complete with my lunch, drinks, a
salmon bass, bits of string, a spring balance, plus other odds
and ends, is left at some convenient place.

Waterproofs

Foul weather gear is something we all know about and
usually carry for most of the time, and on a long fishing trip
it is rarely safe to leave it at home. A really waterproof
jacket—unpadded in summer and padded in spring and
autumn—is essential, and so is a waterproof hat or hood.
But sudden cold is sometimes as unpleasant as pouring rain.
Very cold hands are a problem, and it is difficult to fish in
mitts, and so I am indebted to Roy Buckingham, a great West
Country fisherman, for solving that particular problem. He
wears a pair of ordinary household rubber gloves over a thin
pair of cotton or fine wool gloves. The under-gloves keep
your hands warm while the rubber keeps them dry.

Spinning for Salmon

I would not have you look down on spinning for salmon, but
nor would I have you look up to it either. On certain waters
it has a place, and may well take a fish when a fly would not.
But those who have fished for salmon for many years find
themselves drawn more and more to the fly, and somtimes
will not use any other means of taking a fish, so entranced
are they by that one method. The fly has a pleasure and an
excitement that is unique. Even so, if a man has only one
week a year on a water, and when he comes to it finds it too
coloured for anything but spinning, he is unlikely to sit
and wait.

On most rivers spinning is an alternative to the fly under
certain conditions, mainly the height and colour of the water.
Of course, each fishery has rules, some allow spinning all the

time providing the angler goes down the pool first with a fly, whilst others permit spinning only in difficult places. On certain fisheries it is not allowed until the river reaches a particular height on the gauge, in fact there are so many arrangements that anglers should always make sure of the local rules and conventions.

Spinning Rods and Tackle

There is no need to buy an expensive spinning rod. A simple tubular glass-fibre rod of about 7 ft–8 ft long will do nicely. For most salmon rivers, except the very biggest, a fixed spool reel loaded with about 150 metres of nylon monofilament of about 15 lb breaking strain is adequate. To the end of this line is attached a ball-bearing swivel, a leader point of about 10 lb breaking strain nylon, and the spinner, whatever it may be.

Tucked blood

The end of the nylon is tucked through the first gap next to the swivel and then comes back again to be tucked through the gap in the loop that it has made. This ought to be a very secure knot and it often is. The same knot is used to fasten the nylon to the spinner.

There are hundreds of types of spinners; Devon minnows —often made of wood and therefore needing a lead weight on the leader to take them deep enough; metal or plastic baits which wiggle or wobble through the water, like a Toby spoon, or flashing baits with a spinning vane, like the Mepps. Even with a Mepps it is safer to use a ball-bearing swivel to avoid line kink. When fishing a Devon minnow use two swivels on the link but even this precaution will not always keep the line free of twist.

The problems which arise as a result of line twisting are well known, and the tangles which happen are the bane of the spin-fisher's life, and often result in the loss of expensive equipment.

An old teaspoon bowl, without the handle, drilled at both ends for two split rings, one of which takes the treble hook can be used. The treble is fashionable but a single hook will also do very well in hooking a fish. You can use the handle separately to make a long spinner like a Toby spoon.

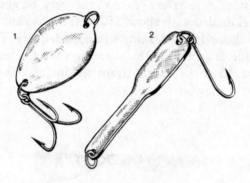

Teaspoon spinners

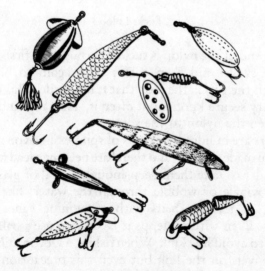

Selection of lures

Spinning can be very effective and even in very coloured water the vibrations of a spinner like the Mepps—fish are very sensitive to vibrations—can take fish in what would otherwise be impossible conditions. But as soon as the water clears at all and the fly becomes visible it is best to change over. In clear water the sight of a spinner can sometimes badly scare a fish. I would not recommend the use of a spinner under clear-water conditions.

Snagging and Otters

Sometimes a good salmon water is full of snags—jutting rocks and old tree stumps in the pools, and even the most careful fisherman can lose half a dozen spinners or more a day. A spoon or minnow can sometimes, though not always, be saved by walking downstream and pulling in the opposite direction to the way it was going when it hit the snag. If various obstructions prevent your getting downstream, then try an 'otter'. This is simply a piece of wood or an old branch fixed on to the line with a piece of string or a clip and allowed to run down the nylon until it gets below the snag. Work the otter as close as possible to the snag before tightening very hard by hand. Never strain the rod tip during an operation of this type.

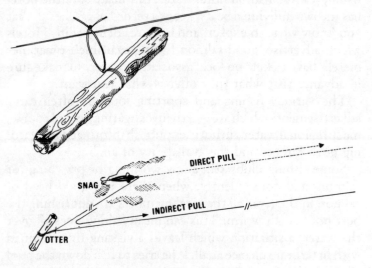

Using an otter

A word of warning. When not using an otter but just pulling at the spinner direct, whether it is snagged in the river or in an overhanging branch, *always* turn your back to it when you pull hard. Keep your face turned away as a spinner, suddenly breaking free, can fly back towards you at an enormous speed.

Where to Fish

Salmon fishing is expensive and difficult to find. Some estate fishing is occasionally advertised and there are sporting agencies who will send you details of vacant lettings. Most salmon beats are let for a week, either with or without accommodation, and the information you recieve regarding waters should include the number of pools, the length of the fishery, transport, keepering, the number of rods allowed, catches for previous years, whether it is fly only, or if and when spinning is allowed, etc. The beat is booked and paid for in advance and money is not refunded. Some anglers insure against unfishable conditions.

Quite often a rod for a day or sometimes for a week can be obtained through the local bailiff or fishery manager of a syndicate or estate or fishing club. *The Field* publishes a guide *Where to Fish* which can be extremely useful. Good fishing can be had on hotel water, but make sure the hotel has its own individual beats, keeps a record of catches so that you know what to expect, and has a resident bailiff. Hotels which advertise 'good salmon fishing available' sometimes merely have tickets on local association water, so make sure in advance that what they offer is what you want.

The various fishing and sporting journals often carry advertisements which are worth investigating, and of course, most regional water authorities publish information regarding both catches and the availability of angling.

Some fishing clubs still allow worming or prawning for salmon, and consequently, when there is a good head of salmon in the river all the local members are out fishing the best pools with worm. This can mean fishing lines all over the water, a situation which leaves a visiting fly fisherman with little or no chance at all. If he tries to fish down the pool when the local members are worming there would probably

'It all went in last time!'

be a stand-up fight. I have seen it happen, so be warned; and this, incidentally, is why bait fishing is never allowed on a well-run fishery. It is too selfish.

But now let us assume you have found your fishing and you are packing your bags, and somewhere, far away and over the distant hills, *Salmo* the Leaper is waiting.

Tactics

A big salmon river seen close to for the first time, especially if you know you have to wade in it, is an awe-inspiring experience. Great cascades of white water burst over the rocks at the head of the pool and torrents flecked with spume go past like a millrace, boiling with the tumult of crossing and conflicting currents. The river may be 50 or 100 metres wide. How can you wade out in such a maelstrom? Where should you stand, where to put your fly?

That is why at first, you must have someone with you who knows the water. A gillie, preferably, who will go with you down the lies. This is not trout fishing, where a skilled angler can find his own fish: this is highly specialized angling. Salmon lies are not always easily found, and even experienced salmon fishermen should welcome local advice on their first visit to a river.

The following diagram illustrates an interesting salmon pool on a medium size river, one which I know well. Assume that it is summer, low water and warm, but the water is going fast. The gillie will indicate a stance out in the fast water at point B. Must you go out as far as that? Oh, yes indeed you must to begin with. I know this pool well and you would not take a fish—not with a fly anyway—unless you did.

The salmon lie in fast water by a ledge and behind an underwater rock in the area C. If you cast to that area from A your fly will be swept away too fast by the strong current. So you wade to point B and cast to C so that your fly moves at a reasonable speed over the lies.

Cast to C1 then C2 and so on. About six or seven casts will cover the lie.

As it is low clear water but running fast, use a floating line and a very long leader—12 ft or more. Use a small fly to start, but if you think this is fishing too high in the water change to a larger one, possibly a size 4. This will fish a little deeper and will be more easily seen.

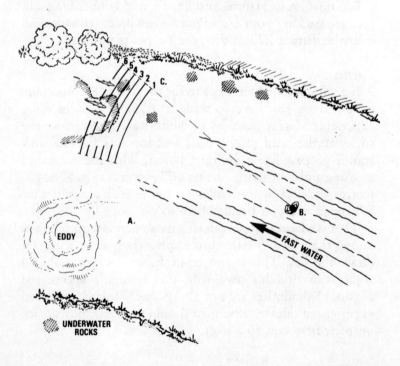

Fish the lies with a floating line and two or three different flies, small and medium, light coloured and dark. If nothing happens, wade out of the water and change your line to a sinker. Put on a very small fly, wade out, and repeat the pattern of casting to C1, C2, and so on.

If you feel a pluck at a larger fly, immediately change to a smaller one and cast to the same place again. A salmon will sometimes be suspicious of a large fly and do no more than just pluck at it, but if offered a smaller version the fish may well take.

If the salmon are dour do not waste too much time on one pool. Move on to the next as a fresh-run fish may be waiting.

If spinning is allowed on the water you might try a cast or two from point A to the area C. With salmon you never know what reaction there might be—salmon are most unpredictable. Spinning across and also upstream can be very effective.

The next diagram illustrates a more complicated situation. Salmon generally lie both in front and also behind a rock that projects from the river. Fishing with a fly, you wade to position B and cast to C1, 2 and 3, to cover the lie in front of the rock.

Once your fly starts dropping around the area C4 it will swing on to the rock. Therefore, fish out C1, 2 and 3 first with two or three different flies on a floating line, or a sinker if you feel like it. Sometimes it is a bore to change lines, but

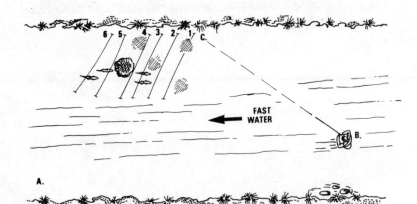

resist the temptation to be lazy. Then, finally, drop your fly
at C5 and 6 well beyond the rock so that the fly swings round
to cover the lies behind it. To remain in contact with the fly
as it swings behind the rock, give the line a 'twitch' and flick
it clear.

Having completed all that is possible from point B, come
out and change to a sinking line and a large fly, a 2 or a 1/0
and go to point A and cast to C5 and 6, stripping the fly back
fast. The upstream fly sometimes works, but remember that
a heavy fly is needed because the current is strong and a small
fly will hardly sink at all before being swept downstream.
Having said this, of course, I now remember that on the
particular pool that I illustrate here, one angler, an American, used a big bushy dry fly on the surface, and a salmon
rose and took.

The pattern of the fly does not, in my opinion, matter very
much, but what does matter I believe, is the weight, size and
tone, and by tone I mean the overall impression—whether
the fly is light or dark—but more about this later.

Meanwhile, let us consider another pool, but under
different conditions. The water is high and running fast,
fining down after a spate, so it is coloured as well. Now
you can forget about a floating line. Use a sinker and big
flies that can be seen—a big black or yellow tube fly, for
example.

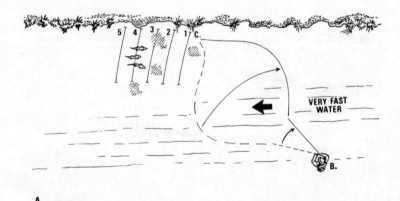

The adjacent diagram depicts a situation in which it must be accepted that B is not a fixed position. The weight of water will determine just how far it is possible to wade. Also, the very fast current will bulge the line downstream, causing what is termed a 'belly' in the line. This belly pulls the fly over the lies too fast. So, when you cast, and the line falls on the water, throw a loop of line upstream with a twirl of the rod, an action called 'mending the line'. This has to be done before the line sinks below the surface, and in time you will find that an upstream mend becomes quite an automatic action—just circling the rod point upstream as the line falls.

This is the kind of water—very coloured and fast—when a spinner comes into its own, either from B, or cast upstream to C1, 2, and 3 from A. Sometimes casting upstream beyond the lies and spinning down fast can be deadly. Occasionally a big heavy tube fly can be fished in the same way, sometimes up, sometimes down, sometimes across and stripped back fast after it has sunk. You must remember—

'. . . there are no certainties in salmon fishing. Every salmon lie in every pool in every river is a separate study in itself. Each lie presents problems to be solved afresh.'*

All this sounds rather confusing to begin with, and indeed maybe it is, but as you go on trying and experimenting you will get what is called 'the feel' of the water. You will look at the way the water moves, the intricate flow of the varying speeds of the water below the surface, how it bubbles here or is sucked down there by unseen obstructions, and you will be able to visualize how your fly will behave in that kind of water, and whether that weight of fly will go deep enough, or whether the water is so warm, low and clear that the salmon can be provoked to rise and take near the surface.

This is part of the fascination of fly fishing and why a man can fish the fly happily day after day without being bored; there are always problems relating to casting and presentation to be solved. Each cast must go where he wants it to go, and each time the fly must act in the way he feels it should. Sometimes it will merely swing with the current,

---

*Falkus and Buller, *Freshwater Fishing*.

sometimes it will be stripped in fast. There are many techniques, and each cast brings its own set of problems, unique to that moment and to that time.

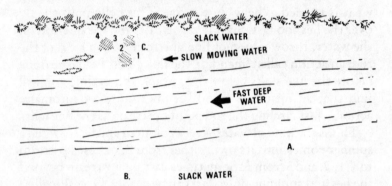

And so on to another pool, and one which needs a great deal of thought before a line is placed on it.

It is high summer and the water is warm, low and clear, and the next diagram indicates that it is too far to cast from A to C, and the fast deep water further out prevents wading. Nevertheless there is a good lie on the far side, and the slow moving water at C is very clear and ideal for a small fly. The angler wades in at B with a floating line and a small fly. But how does he get it to C1, 2 or 3 and what happens if he does?

By 'shooting' the line, and then checking its outward progress suddenly, the line can be made to fall as shown in the next diagram.

The curves in the line will be straightened by the current, and a 'belly' will form downstream. However, before the leader is pulled away, the fly will have travelled towards the salmon just below C4, and then will have moved sideways on, so that they will have had a good look at it—don't forget water is very clear. The next and similar cast goes to C2, and so on. This strange sideways-moving fly just below the water surface may well provoke a salmon's curiosity enough to make it rise and take.

In rivers which are or can be very clear indeed, like the Aberdeenshire Dee, and where the salmon lie in fast water,

they can be taken on a floating fly, but generally only when the water is warm and the river is low. High summer dry fly fishing for salmon has only recently been tried in Scotland where it was introduced by the American angler, Lee Wulff. The technique is essentially the same as dry fly fishing for trout, only the fly is a large bushy lure on a light hook, well-hackled to float. This is cast upstream over the lies, often with a single-handed rod and very light tackle—a leader point of no more than about 6 lb breaking strain.

For wet fly fishing, even though the fly may be only an inch or so below the surface, you do need stronger tackle. A taking salmon in wet fly fishing has the strength of the current with him, and that means a much greater strain on the leader at the moment of the take.

Sometimes in low water fishing at the height of summer, a salmon will move only to very small flies fished a few inches below the surface, and drifted with the current. Very often a take will come as they begin to drag. Sometimes flies are used as small as 10 or 12 with only a wisp of hackle on them. Naturally you use small flies only in clear water conditions. The pattern of fly does not seem to be very important—but we will come to that later.

Meanwhile, consider a weir pool, full of salmon waiting to ascend the fish-pass.

This is a difficult situation because of the turmoil of water. The fish can be almost anywhere, and those by the

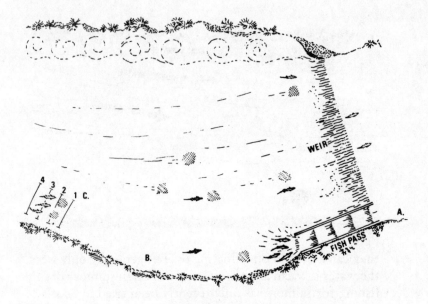

Weir pool

fish-pass waiting to go up are the least likely to take; they are too preoccupied. Start fishing at A, casting across and above the fish which have just ascended the fish-pass and are resting in the slack water in front of the lip of the weir.

Another good place is the tail of the weir pool, fishing from B and casting to C1, 2, 3 and 4. The white water in the middle of the pool is difficult. You can fish it with a fly but you will need a large and very visible one—a big tube fly— and a sunk line, but a spinner will probably do better. In either case it will be mostly luck if you cover a fish, but all the same, weir pool fishing is exciting.

Hook and Take
You can fish for hours, and in some cases for days, and nothing will happen. And then, when you are least expecting it, you will feel your fly snag, or at least it will feel like a snag, that is before the 'snag' moves and you realize, suddenly, that it's a salmon!

When using a single hook, the traditional method of hooking a salmon is to release 2 or 3 feet of spare line as soon

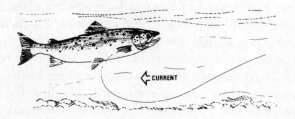

Hooking a salmon

as you feel the fish pull; just drop a loop of spare line which is normally being held between the rod hand and the reel. This causes a loop of line to be pulled by the current downstream of the fish.

A delayed strike will hook the fish firmly in the corner of the mouth, in the place known as the 'scissors', which has the best hooking potential. In practice what generally happens is that the fish pulls and the angler pulls back, but even so, a little extra pressure—a quick heave of the rod— should be exerted as soon as possible to drive the hook in deeply. Remember that a salmon's mouth is mostly bone and gristle. He can often appear to be firmly hooked by the strength of the pull, but if there is not an extra 'strike' the hook can slip and come away.

These things are largely left to an automatic reflex action on the part of the angler, and it is particularly difficult to consider setting the hook correctly when in a matter of a fraction of a second a salmon is on and before you know what is happening the fish is off with a tremedous rush back to the sea. Too many things happen at once. Hang on, keep the rod point high, and try not to obstruct the line as it is being torn off the reel. I remember once that the handle of the reel, turning at speed, hit against the cuff of my sleeve. It was only a gentle knock but the jar was enough to break the leader point by the hook.

If the salmon is heading for rapids there is not much to do except put extra pressure with your fingers on the spool of the reel to try and slow him down. You will either stop him or he will snag and break you. This is where a long rod which keeps the line high is an advantage.

Often a salmon will make a run downstream and then stop in a pool many yards below. He cannot be left there and when you pull at him you are pulling against both the fish and the pressure of the current and he will simply not be moved. If you cannot go downstream and get below, strip off several yards of line, or even more, and allow the spare line to drift below the fish. This exercises pressure from below and may pursuade him to move upstream away from this new restraint, which is, of course, where you want him to be.

Always try to let the fish exhaust himself by fighting the pressure of the current as well as the spring of the rod. Keep him swimming upstream, keep below him, and occasionally put on side strain by lowering the angle of the rod to the river. This pulls him off balance. It all helps.

Never hurry a fish but, at the same time, never let your pressure slacken. A hooked fish can cruise about for hours without exhausting himself too much if he is not under pressure from the spring of the rod.

If the fish jumps, lower the point of your rod until he is

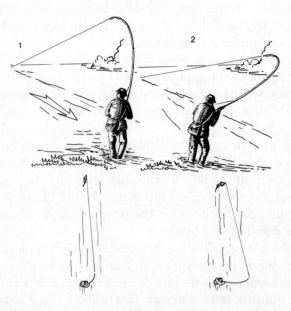

Applying side strain

back in the river. This gives him a little slack so that he is less likely to break the nylon during the leap. In practice a leap may happen too quickly for line to be slackened and then one hopes for the best; and very often everything is all right.

Sometimes a salmon will 'go to ground' and lie doggo in the bottom of a pool. No amount of force will lift him, but one or two well-aimed stones may do the trick. If he is near enough, a jab with a stick or a landing net handle will do; but never allow the fish to rest. If a salmon snags the line the break will mostly be instantaneous; but there are times when he will snag and yet still be on, and in such a case there is not much to be done except to wait and be patient. I have heard of a gillie stripping off and diving in to free line snagged on a sunken log. Such miracles do occur.

Hooking Power
One can lose a salmon in any of a vast number of ways from pulled-out blood knots to a hook that comes away after a fish has taken. Salmon fishermen argue for hours on the merits of various kinds of hooks and their 'power to hold'. There is one theory which says that a treble hook will have at least twice the hooking power of a single, and another theory says that a single hook is undoubtedly the best because it can slip into the 'scissors' far more easily than either a double or treble.

The truth is that a salmon can be well hooked on a single and lightly hooked on a treble and vice versa, and much of it is a matter of chance—I once lost five salmon in succession on trebles—so that if the fish comes unhooked shortly after a take it may well be best to blame the fates rather than the hook. So often a hook will lodge in a piece of gristle that will never hold under more than the lightest of pressures. Use the slightest strain and the fish is lost. Is that the hook's fault?

Netting and Beaching
When the fish is exhausted and begins to drift and lay on its side, that is the time to bring it in. If you are using a net, single-handed, shorten so that the fish is about a rod and a half's length away. Then keep the butt of the rod pressed

Netting

close to your stomach, bend your knees, and the butt of the rod will be supported against the thigh.

The above diagram shows the position for netting. The rod, now held by one hand, the butt supported by the body, is lowered behind the angler and this movement draws the fish towards the waiting net which is just below the surface. If he suddenly shows fight, bring the rod point up at once and slacken or he will break you. This is the danger period but if you have judged it correctly you should be able to slide or glide him to the net. But it is important to remember that a net with a wide gape and a deep purse is essential.

A net of this type will trap the salmon nicely as the rim of the frame is lifted above the water; but do not on any account try to lift the net, with the salmon in it, out of the water. Partly because you may not have the strength to do it, and also because the weight of a thrashing salmon can bend the frame. Drag the net with the salmon to the shallows and take hold of the meshes of the net itself with both hands before the full weight of the fish is lifted from the water.

Next to netting, and often simpler, is beaching. Before fishing a pool look round for a nice level stretch of beach—

mud, gravel or sand—that slopes gently to the shallows. When you have the fish under control and exhausted, walk backwards to the bank and draw him in gently, head first, until he is stranded. If he flaps as he feels the ground it will be too late. The movement of his body or tail will force him further *up* the beach, and within a moment or two he will be helpless.

A stranded salmon can be 'tailed'—that is picked up by grasping the fish with the thumb and forefinger round the body just where it is joined by the tail. There is a bony protuberance at the root of the tail which will prevent the grip slipping. The back of the hand should be towards the salmon's head.

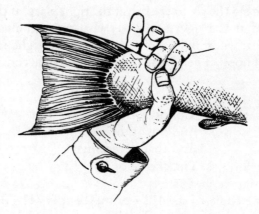

Tailing by hand

But even a 10 lb salmon is quite a weight to lift so you can always hold him by the tail instead of lifting, and stun him with the priest before carrying him with both hands up the bank.

The fish must be killed as soon as possible, which is why you should always carry a priest.

Choosing a Fly
Some fishermen say the rule is you must fish a small fly close

to the surface when the water temperature is above 48°
Fahr, because in water above this temperature the salmon is
generally more active, and therefore more likely to rise to a
fly than in water below 48°. This may be a little fussy, this
precision about degrees, but the principle is right so long as
the water is clear enough for the small fly to be seen. It must
be clear low water and warm.

When the water thickens, rises, or goes faster, you have to
use a heavier fly on your floating line because it needs to be
seen, and it must not skate over the surface of the river, as a
light low-water fly does in fast water.

When the water is cold, salmon can be lethargic and lying
low down, and often the water is fairly cloudy as well, so
then you must use a big fly and a sunk line, possibly a 3 in
tube fly on a weighted tube.

Presenting the fly to the fish at the right place, at the right
time, and at the right speed—is what matters most. This
means that your first choice must be the right size and
weight of hook. Then—and only then—do you consider the
pattern.

> 'Consider the salmon
> And how they lie,
> And that determines
> The choice of fly'

Now we come to the 472—or maybe it is 742—different
named patterns of salmon flies. The patterns are legion, and
everyone has his or her own favourite. Our Victorian
grandfathers swore that the Kelson patterns and none other
had to be used. Not many of them are used nowadays, as
fashions in flies change quickly.

Quite possibly the simplest thing is to fish the pattern
you like the look of and if you are a fly-tier find most
interesting to tie. But people do not like to do this, they
think there must be a *rule* about fly patterns which they
ought to know. In fact there are no rules.

Some say you must use a bright fly on a bright day. This is
based on the very reasonable theory that a natural bait often
looks more brightly coloured when strong sunlight is

Fly presentation. 1 Surface—floating line and small
fly. 2 Floating line, but heavier fly. 3 Water cold
and cloudy, also running fast. Sinking line or even a
fast sinking line with shot pinched on to nylon.

shining on it through the glitter of water. So, on sunny days
on goes a bright little fly, a Shrimp or perhaps a Silver
Doctor to name but two, and they catch fish.

Then the sceptics point out that as salmon do not feed in
fresh water, it does not matter whether the fly suggests a
natural bait or not, as they would not want to eat it in any
case, and as salmon have no eyelids and are often partially
blinded by bright light, a bright fly in dazzling water is not
so likely to be seen as a dark fly. Those who follow this
theory put on a small dark fly in bright clear warm water—
something like a Stoat's Tail. It might take a fish.

The fact is that neither theory is proven. We do not know enough about salmon behaviour to say either what makes them take a lure or which is the best pattern of lure to use. About the only rule that seems reasonable is that the salmon must be able to see the fly. In coloured cold water, when salmon are inclined to hug the bottom and not move from their lies, the fly has to be big and either black—very visible in silhouette—or something startlingly orange or yellow, like a Garry Dog.

For most average fishing, when the river is fining down, the most popular patterns for the moment seem to be darkish flies which have a little brightness or colour or sparkle in places—patterns like the Hairy Mary, Blue Charm and Thunder and Lightning. They are a good compromise.

I know one fine salmon fisherman who uses just one pattern of fly in various sizes—a Shrimp fly—all the season through. Myself, I often tie flies that are of no particular pattern at all, just for the fun of it. In the country, squirrel tails are abundant, and I use them in their natural colour and also dyed in orange and yellow and red for the wings and hackle. These hairwing flies, a mix of coloured fibres, are very simple to tie and they save money. They are not necessarily either better or worse than the intricate Torrish or the elegant Wilkinson.

If you must have a rule about fly patterns then it is best, until such time as we know better, to fish with the one you like the look of. That should serve as well as most.

However, be gentle with other fishermen and do not mock them if they believe that in one part of their river the only pattern worth fishing is a Black Doctor, and in another pool salmon will have nothing but a Parson. They could be right. You may doubt it, but express your prejudices as courteously as you would wish to be treated for your own.

Casting a Fly

This—like doing a fouetté or drawing a bead—is something that can hardly be taught by diagrams or the printed word. The fouetté is a whipping or springing movement and so is the movement of the rod. It is—you must note—the movement of the rod that casts the fly and not the movement of the angler. His task is to move the rod in such a way as to release the power. It is the spring of the rod that moves the line that casts the fly. The angler's task is to flex the rod in the right way and at the right time to create the spring. The angler flexes the rod, and the rod does the rest.

Comparisons are made between flexing a rod and knocking a nail with a hammer. Lift the hammer back. Pause. Hit the nail on the head. Same action with the butt of the rod. Lift. Pause. Hit. There is hardly anything more misleading except when the analogy is used by an expert teacher to correct a fault in the rhythm of flexing the rod. The slow lift of a rod in the back cast followed by the power stroke, the 'flick', is not by any means similar to the upward stroke of a hammer.

One can learn by watching others and by being taught but not by reading. I was self-taught and it took three years before I was able to cast in such a way that I did not feel ashamed. If I had had a good teacher it might have taken three months, and a really expert teacher might have been able to get me up to standard within three weeks—practising for an hour or so every day.

Once the rhythm of flexing the rod is captured, casting is not too difficult, but what is very difficult and even appallingly difficult is to cast accurately and delicately all the time, and to put the fly—in a wind—precisely where you want it to go.

Casting with a double-handed salmon rod of 12 ft or longer is no more difficult—and in fact can be slightly easier—than casting a light trout line on a midge rod. It is a matter of releasing the right amount of muscular power at the right time and to the greatest effect, and though more power is needed to flex a salmon rod, you are, after all, using both hands to do so.

Moreover, with a double-handed rod and a heavier line you can actually feel the pull of the line as it extends itself fully out on the back cast, therefore you know better when to start the forward cast and put in the final forward flick to make the rod flex to the fullest extent. The only difficulty is that the long rod will emphasize and exaggerate the defects of the cast to a greater extent than the single-handed rod. When—for example—the line drops on the back cast because of a loss of power there is so much line out from the double-handed rod, and it is so much heavier than the midge line, that it will drop far more quickly to the ground and snag the fly in the bushes. On the other hand, when the cast is a good one the line will fly much higher than will a midge line, so that you can easily avoid quite tall bushes and trees directly behind the backcast by throwing the line high overhead, much higher than with a single-handed rod.

And—please—never be misled by anglers who talk glibly about casting 30 or 40 yards. I doubt very much whether I have ever hooked a salmon 30 yards away from the tip of my rod and if I have it has been a very rare occurrence, and I have fished the Spey, the Tweed and the Tay and many another quite big river where you would think you would need to cast 30 yards plus. In practice you do not. Many anglers like to boast about their casting prowess, you know, just a little, from time to time, and there is no harm in this providing their friends are tolerant and like them for themselves alone.

Most salmon are hooked within a normal casting distance —15 to 25 yards—and if some pools do need a slightly longer throw then there are breast waders and boats to help you. The reason why it is bad to try for too great a distance when fishing is simply that the angler becomes tense, puts on too much pressure, aerializes too much line with insufficient power to keep up the momentum, and disaster follows.

If you do want to cast 30 yards plus then the best thing is to avoid trying to do so by yourself and take lessons from a tournament caster.

It is advisable, with a double-handed rod, to try to cast with both hands—that is to cast over either shoulder according to the direction of the wind. If you always have your right hand uppermost on your rod and cast over your right shoulder all the time and the wind is coming *from your right* then the fly is likely to be blown slightly towards you on the lift off and to come back still closer to you on the forward cast. This can mean a fly in the back of your head or wrapping itself round your face at a speed of something well

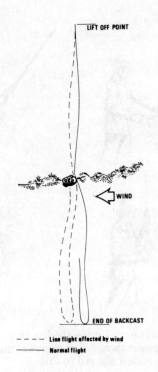

LIFT OFF POINT

WIND

END OF BACKCAST

- - - - Line flight affected by wind
―――― Normal flight

Wind action on casting

over 100 miles an hour. Very unpleasant and to be avoided, even with very small low-water flies.

If the wind is coming to you hard from the right side then put your left hand at the top of the butt and cast over your left shoulder and you will be safe. You may lose a certain amount of distance until you can adjust the rhythm but that is better than a hook in the eye.

One mistake in casting which more or less everyone makes—I do it myself—is to let the rod travel too far back behind the body. This means a great loss of power. One does it without noticing, and then it becomes a habit. If you find yourself getting the habit there is a certain cure. Hold the rod directly in front of your face when you are casting and do not allow it to drift back over your shoulder. Bring the rod right up to the nose.

Casting a floating line is much easier, and in every way more pleasant than casting a sinker. When retrieving a

Two-handed cast. 1 Lifting the line from the water.
2 Start of power flick. 3 End of power flick. 4 Rod
will hit the nose if allowed to drift!

sinker, do not put out too much energy in bringing it back
to the surface of the water to start the backcast. So much
rod power can be expended in this that little power is left to
extend the line adequately in the air. The rod becomes over-
loaded, and sometimes it can even be broken. Bring the line
to the surface slowly and gently, and then, if you need to do
so, roll cast it out downstream. Then you can put in the
power to lift it from the surface to start the backcast.

Always take your time to get the feel of the rod, how it
behaves, how it flexes; acquire this feeling through the
sensitivity of your handhold on the butt, so that you can
sense the rhythm of the movement that transmits energy to
the line. When you have this *feel*, casting will become a joy.

Spin-fishing
Try as I may, I find little to say in praise of casting a spinner.
It is not a subject that provokes the enthusiast in me. You
cannot write about the spinning line floating gently out over

the water as you can with the fly. A spinner does not, in any case, float anywhere. It whips out over the water like a catapult. It buzzes like a bullet from a gun, though nowhere near as accurately.

Having said this, one has sometimes to spin, and that means to cast and get it over with. Once you have the knack of the bale-arm and the grip with the fingers it is fairly unimaginative stuff. The angler flicks the rod out over the water, with an upward flick, and at the same time lets go with the finger holding the nylon, and the spinner flies away, more or less in the right direction.

There is not much more to say except that in spinning the most common fault is to swing the rod from behind the angler in such a way that the casting flick is in a downward direction. The flick should be upwards.

'Not for Covetousness'
To write about salmon fishing only in a practical manner, to discuss flies and tackle, tactics and rods, and little else, is in danger of missing the point. The saying that 'there is more to fishing than catching the fish' may well be a cliché but that does not mean it is less true. To put a fly on the water is an art, a balm, a therapy, an escape to the wilderness from the pressure of cities, a healing of the mind, an adventure, an excitement of the spirit. There is also another consideration that will affect our attitude and our outlook, our whole philosophy if you like.

The Atlantic salmon is a threatened species. The stock has been reduced, noticeably, in a lifetime—by over-netting, especially illegal netting on the high seas, by disease and pollution from chemicals, fertilizers and industrial waste. By the latter half of the last century nearly half the salmon rivers of England had been destroyed by industrial and domestic effluents. The Thames was once one of the best salmon rivers in Europe, and the Tyne and the Tees had huge runs of fish. Look at them all today. Throughout the whole of western Europe the salmon rivers have been dying. There are hopeful signs that at last the process is being halted. But even so the overall salmon stocks are near danger level.

It is easy for the fly fisherman to blame everyone but himself and to do little more than grumble. It is hardly enough. He should at least be a member of organizations fighting for the preservation of fisheries such as the Salmon and Trout Association, the Atlantic Salmon Research Trust, the Freshwater Biological Association, and the Anglers' Co-operative Association.

The fly fisherman needs also a certain amount of discipline for himself. There is a minority—but it may be a sizable minority—who have become killers. If they take a brace in a day they want more. If they take two brace they want more still. They go on killing. They will never think of putting back a hen fish full of spawn. It is kill and kill and the surplus can be sold to pay for the cost of the beat and the hotel, for travel and expenses.

The truth is that fly fishing can only be enjoyed to the full if it is kept separate from the market place. The intangibles which cannot be costed are those that matter most. It has all been said many times before, but perhaps never so well or clearly than by the unknown author of the *Treatysse of Fysshynge Wyth An Angle* 500 years ago:

> 'You must not use this artful sport for covetousness, merely for the increasing or saving of your money, but mainly for your enjoyment, and to procure the health of your body and more especially of your soul.'

CHAPTER FIVE

About Sea Trout Fishing

Conrad Voss Bark

Scientists tell us that sea trout belong to the same species as brown trout even though they are migratory fish and look and behave very much like salmon, and indeed a big sea trout looks so much like a salmon that they are not easy to tell apart. The quickest way to differentiate between them is to look at the tail.

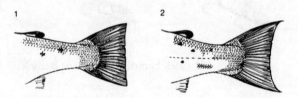

1 Sea Trout's tail: straight edged and sometimes even convex. 2 Salmon's tail: forked and with slight points on the tips.

Summer nights in June, July and August are the best for sea trout fishing. Young fish on their first run up river are known by different names in various regions—sewin, herling and peal are some of them—and they average about a pound in weight. A good sea trout is a 5-pounder, and anything over 10 lbs is a very good fish indeed. In Norway they run even bigger.

The habits of sea trout vary from region to region, even from river to river. Local knowledge—as with salmon—is essential. They come up river, sometimes singly but mostly in shoals of varying size, and rest in certain pools which are usually known. Again, like salmon, the sea trout do not eat

on their spawning run and once they leave the estuary it is
unusual to find food in their stomachs.

But, unlike salmon, a sea trout in a river will rarely take a
fly during the day, only occasionally, and the time to fish for
them is mostly from dusk to dawn. Some years they will be
very active in the pools at night and take eagerly. Other
years they will run fast and dour to the spawning grounds
with hardly a look at a fly. They are strangely shy creatures.

Hugh Falkus, on the Cumbrian Esk, developed methods
of fishing for them which cover most of the regional
variations. Before midnight he will fish with a low-water
salmon fly on a floating line, but if that does not work he will
change to a large streamer lure on a sunk line. There are
other variants: a small fly on a double hook, a maggot fly—
beloved of the Welsh—and a 'wake lure'. Falkus's wake lure

Various flies. 1 Cork bodied. 2 Palmer or Bumble.
3 Parachute.

is not much more than a large cork on a tandem hook. Palmer
flies and parachute flies can also be used. When the trout are
splashing in the pools the lure is thrown across and allowed
to drift downstream, and then dragged back over the surface
causing a wake. The method at times can be deadly, and at
other times will be no use at all.

That, of course, is what sea trout fishing is like. The fish
are highly nervous in fresh water and their behaviour
changes not only from year to year but from night to night.
Hardly any night is ever the same.

Rods and Lines
A good strong trout rod—cane, carbon or glass—is all you
need. It should not be too stiff as sea trout have soft mouths
and have to be treated gently. If you fish small rivers an 8 ft

6 in rod will be good enough but for larger rivers and boat
fishing on lochs a 10 ft rod is better. Falkus, on the
Cumbrian Esk, carries two 10 ft rods, one loaded with a
sunk line and the other with a floater. In some of the small
Devon rivers, however, a sunk line is unnecessary because it
will cause the fly to snag on every cast. Adjust your tackle
to the rivers you fish.

Flies
Almost any fly will sometimes take a sea trout, and
sometimes almost any fly will not. They are moody things.
As with salmon, rely above all else on local knowledge and
methods and flies. A low-water salmon fly of almost any
pattern on hook size from 8 to 4 is a good standby to start
with, but after that you can go to a 3-inch tube, a size 10 blue
and silver traditional pattern, a wake lure, a popper bug or a
worm fly, and still not know why they will take one and not
the other. Sometimes sea trout will take a dry fly in bright
sunshine during the day, but it does not happen often. The
night is best.

   Most nights when I go down to the river I will have on a
10, 8 or 6 traditional single hook pattern of fly—a hairwing
dressing—and maybe change to a larger low-water salmon
fly later. If the fish are moving frequently in the pools—that
big splash, splosh, splash which is so exciting to hear at
night—then I will use a parachute fly on a dropper as a wake
fly and fish it on a greased leader. When the sea trout are
really 'on' the wake lure they will often look at little else.
One has to find out these things either from the locals or by
experiment.

Night Fishing
One thing you can do at night is to fish with strong nylon.
You can use a nylon point of 10 lb or stronger if you wish. It
helps when you have a smash take. It also helps when you
want to pull your fly out of a bush on the opposite bank:
   It is essential to carry on you:—
      A fly box with a variety of different flies
      Spare spools of nylon or made-up spare casts
      Scissors

A priest
A landing net—large trout-size on a sling
A trout bass or bag to carry the fish
A wading stick—useful even if you are not wading
And a good reliable torch.

On the subject of torches, these can be slung on string round the waist or kept in a pocket but one of the best

'Flexlite' pocket torch

torches for sea trout fishing is a little gadget used originally in America, but now available in England. It clips on the pocket firmly and the bulb head is on a flexible neck which can be moved in any direction. It is admirable for changing flies and seeing where you are walking in the dark.

River Tactics
Before you go to a pool at night explore it during the day. If possible get someone who knows the pool to go with you. Wading at night can be very dangerous indeed. Also, you need to see in daylight where the fish are lying. In clear water they can be seen; in coloured water you need to know where they are likely to be.

Sea trout will begin to move just before dusk. If you are

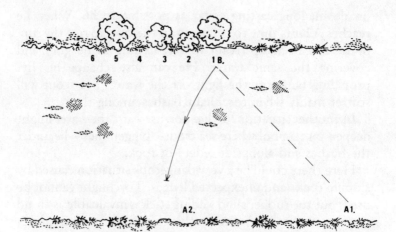

very careful you can begin to fish for them then, providing
the water is coloured. On a clear water stream you should
wait until it is nearly dark otherwise they will see you and be
frightened. Sea trout will often move up to the head of a
pool at night, lying behind rocks in quite fast water.

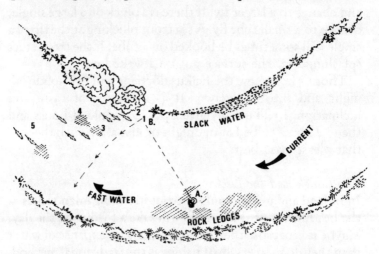

On this fast run, rocky and with white water, the angler
starts at A1 and wades down to A2. Wading is safe only
between these two points so he has to make the best of it.
He casts his fly across to B1 and lets it swing in the current.
He retrieves slowly and lifts off carefully as a sea trout will
often follow the fly and take it just before lift off. He fishes

on down, long casting as far as possible to B6. When he reaches A2 it is time to come out of the river to rest the run, or he can back upstream to A1, casting as he goes and covering the same water. He can also change his fly, providing he keeps the light off the water. Sea trout will scatter madly when torchlight flashes among them.

In another situation further downstream, the water might deepen into a pool where sea trout—bigger ones—lie under the bushes and alongside ledges of rock.

Here there could be a very dangerous situation caused by sloping rocks and unexpected ledges. Torchlight cannot be used, but the rubber shod wading stick is invaluable as an aid to get out to point A. Stay at this point and cast to B1 and 2, and then B3, 4 and 5.

When casting to B5 the line is almost directly downstream, and the fly can be moved from side to side in the current by swaying the rod tip. Big fish are taken this way.

Start with a small fly—a size 8 sea trout fly—and if nothing happens back out of the water, go behind a bush, and change to a larger fly. If there is a pluck on a large single, change to a small tube fly. A sea trout plucking at the tip of a single will sometimes be hooked on a tube. If the trout start splashing near the surface put on a wake lure.

Those who follow the Falkus doctrine will fish solidly all night and into the dawn. It is a matter of taste and inclination. I will usually give a pool a couple of hours and then be home to bed at midnight or just after. Fish the way that pleases you best.

The Lough and the Loch

In Ireland and in Scotland sea trout in the big inland lakes— the headwaters of the rivers—will take a fly during the day. Maybe it is because they feel safer in a large expanse of water than they do in rivers. Boat fishing is the traditional method, with two anglers drifting downwind and throwing a team of flies, often quite small flies, into the likely places, along the edges of reefs, inshore into bays and weed beds, and along the track of river currents.

In Ireland, sea trout are called white trout—another of their numerous local names—and are mostly taken on mayfly imitations, and bumbles fished on or close to the surface. Sunk or deep water fishing is often done with no more than a large spinner trailed on a nylon line behind the boat.

In Scotland, the traditional flies are the Peter Ross, the Teal, Blue and Silver, and the Mallard series, generally fished as a team of two or even three flies from a boat on a drift. Brown trout and salmon are often taken during forays of this sort, so that in some ways this is not specifically sea trout fishing, but fishing for any game fish that is likely to move a fly.

Sea Pool Fishing

It is exciting fishing for herling, whitling or finnock (local names for sea trout) in places such as Argyll and Kintyre—and many others too—where small rivers run down into a little estuary on the shore. The sea trout, large and small, congregate in the estuary before starting their run upstream. A tiny sea pool from a small stream not more than a few yards wide will often hold fish of a pound or more, and they will take a fly freely about an hour before and after high tide when they are freshly in from the sea. They are fished for with a floating line, a long leader and small traditional flies on hook sizes from 12 to 8 or 6.

The pool may look empty, but as the flies swing round in the current a trout will shoot up from the cover of seaweed, snatch the fly, turn and go down again and will be back in the weed so fast it is just like seeing a silver flash in the water, and no more.

The technique is really just like river fishing—wet fly down the run of the tide instead of downstream—but when the water goes slack at high tide you can either wait for the next movement of current to begin, or else throw the flies out as though you are fishing a lake and retrieve them slowly by hand.

Keep out of sight, and even if the pool looks empty there will suddenly be that flash of silver, a lightning take, and the fish is on, hooking himself against the pressure of the current on the line.

When the day is over, your rod, line and reel, and indeed

all your tackle must be washed carefully in clean fresh water
to remove the brine. Salt can corrode metal fittings on
fishing tackle in a matter of a few hours, so nothing must be
left unwashed overnight.

The Fish is On

A big sea trout will fight furiously, leaping like a rainbow,
and though there is not much difficulty in leading them to
the net when they are hooked during the day—though even
then they will break you if given half a chance—at night it is
a different matter. In the darkness the take feels like an
explosion—a violent bang on the rod and the scream of the
reel. On a dark night you may well have no idea where the
fish is except by looking up to see which way your rod is
bending. The silhouette against the sky will tell you.

But even on a very dark night you will see the white gleam
of the fish as he rolls on his side, exhausted; and not until
then is it possible to slide him towards the net.

If you hook a sea trout when you are wading deep in a river
on a dark night it is best to play the fish right out from where
you stand without moving. When the trout is safely netted
the angler, using his wading stick, can then make his way to
the bank; or if he likes he can kill the trout by holding it in
the meshes of the net and hitting it on the head with his
priest. When it is dead, it is safe to take it out of the net,
unhook it, and slide it into a bass carried on a belt or string
round the waist. To avoid dropping the fish back into the
river, keep a grip all the time, with one finger in its mouth or
its gills.

To do all that, of course, you will need to use both hands.
The easiest way to park your rod is down the top of one of
your waders; and as long as the reel goes down, the rest of
the butt will follow. There are fishing jackets with loops
and straps to hold a rod, and these are admirable, but
somehow I never seem able to find the loop in the dark.

The Night is Lonely

Fishing at night can be a frightening business, especially for
city dwellers who do not know the wild. A cow breathing in
the darkness on the other side of a bush can rouse the most

superstitious awe and terror. Our instinct is to be afraid of the dark and the unknown, and when we go fishing—to quote Howard Marshall—we 'shake hands with the cave-man'. A warm summer night with the moon rising, mist coming over the river, a rustle of something strange behind us, and before we know where we are we are looking nervously over our shoulder.

Fish, if you can, with a good companion. It gives a certain comfort if you know someone else is on the pool above, and in practical terms it could be a godsend if either one of you were to fall and sprain an ankle, or worse. Take very warm clothing, and a flask of something if you are going to fish after midnight.

Sea trout fishing in those three months of summer nights is exciting and exhilarating—quite unlike fishing either for salmon or non-migratory trout. It has a quality all of its own, and that fine Irish writer, T. C. Kingsmill Moore, had the heart of the matter in his book *A Man May Fish*:

> '. . . The value of night fishing is as a sedative to fretted nerves and a tired brain. A sedative, yet something more, a portal of escape from the instancy of the present. As the night deepens the river takes command. Its voice mounts, filling the valley, rising to the rim of the hills, no longer one voice but a hundred. Time and place are dissolving; the centuries have lost their meaning; timelessness is all. One foot is crossing the invisible frontier which bounds the land of the old gods . . .'

That captures some of the magic.

CHAPTER SIX

The Future of the British Salmon Fisheries

Gilbert Hartley, BSc, MIBiol, DipRMS, FZS

From what was said in the analysis of the present condition of salmon in Britain, it will be recognized that the continuing presence of the fish in our fauna depends on avoiding any further stresses on its environment and on the fish stock. Its natural resources may be regarded as being stretched to their limit, so that any increase in pressure on them would result in a very real danger of collapse.

It has been pointed out that a difficulty in salmon conservation in Britain is that a number of different authorities have control of individual factors affecting the issue, often without any stated responsibility for fisheries apart from a benevolent neutrality.

Where anything is controlled by committees, assembled from authorities mainly concerned with some separate activity, it is usual for each of the authorities to consider that the inter-departmental deliberations cannot be allowed to interfere with its more central planning. Water supply, land drainage, pollution, and navigation all represent tangible assets of known financial weight, to be protected in preference to fancy fishing of little relative worth. It seems, therefore, that the survival of salmon in this still United Kingdom may eventually be resolved on a regional basis according to local legislation. In this, Scotland has the advantage that salmon is well established as a valuable commerce, and that Scottish law has reflected this.

However, in England, salmon suffers under the disability of representing an élite preoccupation, and therefore something to be handicapped in comparison with a true 'people's fish' such as cod or roach.

Another difficulty in estimating the viability of the British salmon is the delay which occurs between the incidence of a stress and the demonstrable effect. In combination with unreliable statistics, this is exceedingly dangerous.

In recent years, the drift-net fishery for salmon off the north-west coast of Ireland has increased unchecked; the stock which is being ravaged by this activity is unidentifiable. It was this indiscriminate predation by coastal nets around Scotland which led the Hunter Committee to recommend that commercial salmon capture should be confined to traps in rivers, where the local stock could be rationally cropped, as nets adjacent to west-coast rivers caught fish *en route* for the whole eastward coast of Scotland and England and even Norway.

At present, famous rivers are starved of fish, but nobody can rationalize the cause, so that the blame is laid on foreigners ring-netting on the high seas. This may or may not have some substance, but where the missing fish are grilse, it is appropriate to look more closely at hand. This is an example of a stress requiring legal correction, and of one where legal redress is unlikely to occur because other considerations take precedence.

On the basis that a wild salmon stock is likely to be decimated without remedy, commercial interests are increasingly turning to the prospects of ranching salmon—leaving them to feed in controlled areas from which they can be removed at an appropriate time for the market.

The process was first employed by the Vik brothers in Norway, using pumps to drive sea water through cages of growing fish, but has now been taken up with at least biological success by a number of groups working in the west of Scotland, using the tidal streams to wash fixed cages in which the fish swim. Recruitment is from artificially reared smolts, so that it must be expected that within twenty years, selective breeding will produce a race of salmon adapted to life in these conditions.

From the precedent of Professor Donaldson at Seattle, it should be possible to develop a strain having a very high conversion factor and a very high growth rate. The practicability of such a plan would depend on the ecomomics of the venture, in particular the availability of food at a realistic price, and this is the aspect which must cause the greatest concern in the long run, owing to the mounting pressure against the use of foodstuffs to produce animal protein.

Fish nutrition is a subject of special study, and with the precedent of the use of chicken manure as a cattle-feed, there is no shortage of possibilities. With the geographical advantages of the Scottish west coastal topography, the Gulf Stream and a traditional familiarity with fixed nets, quite apart from experience developed in connection with large engineering structures for the North Sea, this ought to prove a certain success for those concerned, and offers auxiliary opportunities for the culture of oysters and mussels.

The improvement in river quality has had the effect of restoring several large rivers to the salmon habitat. The Tyne, as mentioned earlier, has never quite lost the stock which made it formerly the chief salmon river in England, and mechinical restoration of the situation caused by gravel extraction will, in the absence of fresh encroachment, restore its fecundity. The water transfer scheme and Kielder reservoir have been planned with the development of the salmon stock firmly in mind.

The Severn has retained a good stock of fish and, apart from local pollutions which follow the general pattern of being ameliorated as obsolete plant is replaced and better standards enforced, its main troubles have been due to obstructions. Some of these were defended from improvement for decades on the score that those responsible for them could not afford either to build passes or abandon the weir for demolition.

The advent of Water Authorities, with a more extensive remit than the previous River Authorities, represents a distinct gain in this connection, though the administrative grouping of the Severn with the Trent as a single Authority is less welcome. In this case, a salmon river of great size and with local peculiarities is attached to a very large river with traditionally powerful interests in coarse fishing. Though the option to re-open the Trent to salmon if the possibility occurs has been retained, and a pass installed at Cromwell weir during reconstruction some years back, in present circumstances coarse fishing is the financially dominant partner everywhere, and coarse fishing interests must be preferred for the sake of financial equity.

Apart from the disparate nature of the fishery interests, extremely large organizations contain a self-constricting element. We have passed from the Fishery Board situation where an unpaid Fishery Officer with a staff of some four poorly-rewarded bailiffs attempted to maintain the fisheries of half a dozen small rivers without incurring any expense in the process, to a state where Fisheries is a single facet of an integrated Scientific Services Department with its own Director, Assistant, and Deputy, with supporting staff including a Chief Fisheries Officer and local Fishery Officers, each having a staff of a few bailiffs.

Though notionally each local group is backed by the full constructional might of the Authority's Works Department, in general it is as difficult to secure a place in the queue for attention as it used to be to persuade a local contractor to do a job on his day off for a nominal fee.

Conditions of service have improved, but it would be interesting to have a comparison between the numbers of men actually on the riverside or in the river now, and twenty-five years ago. There is no question about the increase in complication.

The improvement in the condition of the tidal compartment of the Thames has very properly been publicized, and the project of re-establishing a salmon run mooted. It is worth examining this in some detail.

Historically, the Thames was a famous salmon river, and must have been originally at least as good as the Tyne. With the advantage of a southern climate, it may well have resembled the Test, producing one-year old smolts and receiving large spring fish. There are no natural obstructions to the running fish, and the water is rarely cold enough to hold fish back if there were. (The frozen Thames in London was by no means an annual happening, and the passage of old London Bridge would have presented no problem at high tide.)

Human obstruction, by weirs for trapping fish and milling, culminated in the installation, during the last three hundred years, of a series of forty-four weirs designed to provide navigational depths, thus altering the nature of the river from a flowing stream to a series of pools like a gigantic fish-pass. In the earlier stages of the process, salmon still entered the river, and we may be certain that the weirs were constructed with this in mind. However, for the past century and more, no salmon have entered, owing to the state of the tidal compartment, while the demands of commerce and the possibilities open to engineers have developed rapidly.

The consequence has been that the weirs have become structures designed to retain water and to release floods without regard to fish passage. This could in principle be rectified at a cost, but what will be far more difficult to restore are the lost spawning grounds of the salmon. In place of a relatively shallow flow over gravel which must have provided suitable areas, the river now consists of a steady deep channel having many characteristics of a canal. Whether salmon could spawn in the main river in sufficient numbers to maintain a stock must be open to doubt, and at least initially it will be necessary to manage weir streams, and other apparently suitable channels to provide spawning ground.

The scale of a re-stocking operation is enormous if the species is to be given a real chance of maintaining itself. There is no such thing as a small-scale pilot experiment, as the necessity is that the salmon should be able to swamp the opposition, and return in numbers adequate to maintain their position.

Consider a pair of ten-pound fish on the spawning ground. Taking a figure of 50 per cent for fishing success, these represent four entering the river. Smolt-tagging experiments show that on nights when large numbers migrate, 4 per cent would be an optimistic return rate; with an initially low stock, 1 per cent would be reasonable. This means that to get two fish on the redds, we have to start by releasing 400 smolts, and have no marine accidents.

Between the hatching egg and the migrant smolt it is usual

to allow a survival of 0.1 per cent, so that 400,000 ova are required to produce one pair of fish. Quite obviously this is not a realistic life table, as a 10-pound fish will lay some 8,000 eggs, and on the computed basis could not maintain the species; at some point the population passes a critical level above which the returns become more favourable, particularly in the matter of smolts returning as adults.

An initial stocking aimed at providing fifty pairs of fish would therefore need to comprise 20 million eggs—a number difficult to obtain, and which would require artificial incubation because the spawning areas are hypothetical. It would be easier to start by using artificially-reared smolts, reducing the numbers to 20,000.

In Sweden, where all salmon are artificially propagated because the rivers are developed for electrical generation, it is reckoned that smolts retained for two weeks in a given river will home to that one and not their hatchery. In a case such as the Thames, smolts could be reared in a station, far up the river, from the fry stage, and transported down river, as they showed an inclination to migrate, in enclosed cages or skeleton boats to avoid predation in fresh water.

With the main river probably useless for spawning to the extent required for supporting a population, the tributaries would have to be relied on extensively from the start, and indeed a fish has been recovered from the Kennet already.

While it is a matter of anxious hope that the species may again establish itself in the Thames, and fulfil the ambition expressed to the Press at the time when the Salmon and Freshwater Fisheries Laboratory was opened in Westminster in 1948, it is worth looking wider afield.

The Pacific salmon, of which there are five species closely adapted to particular categories of river, are capable of spawning successfully in deep water, and even in lakes where there is an outflow of water from the submerged gravel. While of little account for angling, they are extremely valuable in commercial fishing, and are caught by trolling in the sea as they approach the river mouths. There is a case for considering the introduction of Pink salmon (*Oncorhynchus gorbuschka*), otherwise known as the Humpback, which was introduced by the Russians into the rivers of the Kola

Peninsula. Normally, Pacific salmon are intensely fixed, not only to their native river, but to a fixed part of it, and enter at an exact time of year, so that facilities can be brought into use for a short period only, but the Kola river Humbacks were caught in Northern Norway, and a few in British waters. Whether the initially promising introduction in the Kola region actually 'took' or not is uncertain.

A feature which the Humpback salmon shares with the Chum, and a large proportion of the Chinook salmon, is that the fry start migrating to sea very soon after emerging from the gravel. They are thus relatively easy to sustain in the river, but more subject to predation in the sea, owing to their small size.

While no-one would willingly allow these exotic species to compete with our domestic salmon, in the present position of shortage of traditional fish of every description, and the deleterious alteration of water courses for maintaining an expanding human population, it would be quixotic to refuse recognition to the part they could play in replacing Atlantic salmon where the native species has been disinherited.

It goes without saying that such an introduction, like any other essay in acclimatization, requires the most stringent biological examination in advance. In the case of an introduced salmonid there is only a remote risk of the alien ousting a native stock, but there is a risk of permitting the successful invasion of exotic parasites or viral strains, with catastrophic consequences, or of promoting a familiar nuisance to the status of a dangerous pest. Atlantic salmon from Europe and America mingle to some extent, as do Pacific salmon from America and Asia, but although Pacific salmon have been introduced to the Great Lakes in the eastern watershed of America, it would require a positive clearance before their contact with British trout in British rivers could be regarded as free from the danger of producing disease carriers or exploiting some lack of resistance to infection.

The responsibility for investigating this problem, and the host of other problems which comprise salmon conservation must fall on a properly equipped and competent organization with both the time and the means to investigate them exhaustively, and it is here that this country is weak at present.

Elsewhere, the usual arrangement is for there to be an Institute of Freshwater Fisheries, (to which coastal fisheries are often attached). Such an organization comprises a permanent body of specialists and budding experts in all the multifarious disciplines and along all the margins where two or more adjoin. The individual flair of the inmates will range from the purely abstract to the utterly practical, the same individual often showing extremes of both in his handling of various facets of different projects.

In Britain, the position until lately has been that freshwater fishery research in England and Wales was carried out by scientists acting as Inspectors of Salmon and Freshwater Fisheries in the Ministry of Agriculture, Fisheries and Food, by scientists belonging to the independent Freshwater Biological Association, by scientists working for the Water Pollution Research Laboratory, and by various academic departments. In Scotland, the inspectorial and scientific duties are separated; oddly enough, before the war they were combined in Scotland and virtually separated in England.

There are serious defects in the total arrangement. It is evident that with different legal systems in England and Scotland, a different inspectorial system is reasonable to regulate different Fishery Acts. With the present emphasis on Welsh devolution, a third group will also be required. But there is nothing but loss to all concerned in the fragmentation of the scientific work on a nationalistic basis. This involves the provision of largely duplicated facilities, with the perpetual danger that one or other of the controllers will bend his energies to scoring off his rival rather than promoting the search for knowledge. This is not a flight of fancy; it was in times now past a vital factor in the conduct of research.

At the present time there is confident collaboration between the scientists—as indeed there is between British and foreign salmon specialists—but the inspectorial connection on the English side, which has kept the laboratory uniquely anchored in Whitehall to its grave disadvantage, means that a programme of work is always liable to disruption by sudden requirements.

A single homogeneous organization with both the variegated competence and manpower to deal with normal emergencies, and commensurate laboratory facilities, is in a stronger position than two separate small ones; sudden eventualities are the stimulating leaven of fishery workers. But whereas they merely provide a topical interest for members of a large group, they completely disrupt a small one, which may have to cancel an arrangement with outside parties and lose an opportunity which will not recur for a year, and this reduces the confidence of the outside individuals, who are usually very experienced where fish are concerned, in the basic competence of the scientists.

The need to secure and maintain public support and confidence is fundamental in salmon research, and requires both practicality and diplomacy. The latter is of particular importance as friction is almost inevitable.

It must be recognized that there is a certain antagonism between the various persuasions of anglers, who tend to adopt a defensively hostile attitude towards any concession granted to rivals, and also a frankly lunatic fringe which equates all fishery management with violation of a state of pristine abundance.

Some years ago an outraged angler had a letter published drawing attention to the obscene activity which had resulted in the fish he had caught having been reduced to the humiliation of going around carrying a number. This was instantly supported by a second agreeing that the power-mad moguls of Whitehall could not stomach the idea of any mortal thing living unregulated.

This is not really more absurd than the demand which used to be a perennial feature at gatherings of salmon anglers, that the Authorities should solve the old problem of whether like bred like; it would only involve fertilizing ova from a summer fish with sperm from spring and summer cock fish (and vice versa), and seeing how the smolts returned in the next generation. Lifetimes have passed while scientists fight to get a reliable answer to far simpler problems, like the timing of smolt runs or the ratio of brood stock to smolt run, any of which tie up the entire research facility and annual budget, and may be ruined by a freak flood at any stage.

In fact, research work on salmon problems is not a matter to be solved simply by adequate funding, though this is an essential preliminary. The true expert gets more information from the brook he passes on his way to the laboratory than many of his senior colleagues could extract from an expensive planned programme, complete with computer. There is an individual dedication, amounting to a calling, which is not revealed at interviews, but which leads men to spend the night waist deep in a freezing river for months on end, and the highly-integrated administrative structure appropriate to highly funded research in laboratories tends to frustrate folk whose fish will react immediately to a local storm 400 miles from authority on a Saturday night.

No amount of time spent in inter-departmental study groups co-ordinating joint involvement in projects attracting multilateral co-operation will ever produce results as complete and rapid as a single group of workers who have all the strings in one set of hands. It is possible that devolution may bring us to the Canadian situation, where there is provincial control of sport and conservation, but salmon are a federal responsibility. It is a system which works.

In summation, the practical requirements are quite simple, and do not involve any extra organization. The most difficult commodity to produce—the experienced manpower—exists already. What is required is the opportunity for this existing expertise to get to work with the advantage of, instead of in spite of, its facilities.

Control of everything pertaining to freshwater fisheries except the bare legalistic framework has passed from the Ministry of Agriculture, Fisheries and Food to the complex at present denominated the Department of the Environment. In particular, the waters of the country are now regarded primarily as potential stuff for supplying taps. The Fishery Departments of the Water Authorities provide a local and invaluable check to deteriorating conditions, but they are a fragmented force, requiring the support of a unified body in a position to provide the general answers to specific questions. These answers cannot be obtained by funding University research because University research projects have in practice to be capable of completion in two years' experiment and one year's analysis, while salmon research inevitably runs into decades.

What is desperately needed is a single properly equipped salmon research institute, situated in its area of action, with adequate space to construct temporary field works, and a safe water supply. Proximity to a University is desirable. There would be a good pratical case for a British Institute sited in the Tweed valley, serving both Scotland and England in a biological, not a political capacity. It would be centrally situated, uncluttered, and with good communications. The Freshwater Biological Association has shown that pure research can flourish in seclusion; an Institute engaged in applied research not very far off, and surrounded by a ring of Universities traditionally involved in its sphere, would be a logical corollary.

Index